This heat, it's hell closing in on me...

by

James S M Parker

Grosvenor House
Publishing Limited

This book is published by
Grosvenor House Publishing Ltd
28-30 High Street, Guildford, Surrey, GU1 3EL.
www.grosvenorhousepublishing.co.uk

A CIP record for this book
is available from the British Library

ISBN 978-1-78623-724-8

Introduction

How do I explain this book without giving away too much? **Is it a direct follow up to my first book 'Love or Suicide and the Life In-between'?** Yes it is, despite there being a good 12 years between the writing of the two. **What is it about?** Well, where 'Love or Suicide...' was about an instant response to a period in my life, this book is about the inner struggle and complete lack of dealing with that period. Despite the happy and content life I was leading from 2005, something inside me broke in 2013. This led to severe depression, lack of any sleep, self-harm, prescribed drugs and finally counselling sessions. This story is woven in with my poetry about the subjects of Life and Death and is part one of 'this heat, it's hell closing in on me'. Part two was born from my desire to write every day for a year and keep a diary so is a combination of these two desires. A 2014 diary written in poetry/short story form using many different styles and littered with the odd photograph. Finally the epilogue is a little taster of what I am working on next...or rather what I am working on now. 14/02/16.

"of course the darkness will always be there,
it will never go – but it will never win"

(Our very DNA is made up of our Mother and Father. They are the ones that shape us into the person we will become through the most influential years of our lives and onwards into the future. We are them and they live on in us...always)

My Mother is in my heart. Her kindness and empathy makes up the best of me. I listen, I understand, I help and I never take anything for granted. I am proud to have been her son and for her to have been my mother...if I could have taken her pain away and banish her disease then I would have sacrificed everything to do so...even my own life.

As for my Father, he is in my head. I have tried exiling him from me with ink. I have tried drowning him from me with alcohol. I have tried cutting him from me with blades. I have tried talking him from me with words. I have tried urging him from me with feelings. I have tried silencing him from me with sleep. I have tried beating him from me with fists. And yet he remains, just there, just out of reach, just out of sight...just out of touch; a forever ghost that continues to haunt me.

contents

prologue – (or just a man) vii

this heat, it's hell closing in on me –
part 1 (or 'Life and Death and the Life In-Between') 1

this heat, it's hell closing in on me –
part 2 (or 'two zero one four') 49

epilogue – (or K.A.R.A.) 343

thanks – (or inspirations) 344

prologue

just a man

a feeling shared by those
the hurt felt by some
or race suffers in sorrow
the select few suffers in suicide
their despair blinds
their loneliness chokes
their pain scars
their souls broken.

just a man to feel loss
just a man to think dark
just a man to push limits
just a man to tip over...
...just a man to express
just a man to pour out
just a man to see the light
just a man to create.

that book revealed all
a fill for my void
pages of recovery (**not quite**)
words of honesty
not of glorification
but of victory (**short lived**)
an empty note (**for now**)
now, a full life (**it isn't over**)

(and so we meet again, lost in emotion and ink and life and death

for............)

THIS HEAT, IT'S HELL CLOSING IN ON ME...

Part One

This is...

Visions of light to signal a whole new beginning
Thrust from within, cries shed a rainbow
Tears that will never be so honest again
This game to begin, this legacy to be left
As twisted rules form and break each other
And the innocence of youth is boxed, a sadist
This prospect of old age always hiding in full view
Amongst a land of metal and glass
The hand held book an old fossil perverted into code
A code that guards the graveyard of past simplicities
And lays waste to anything living and breathing
Eaten from the inside out, trampled and worn
Horizons ignored in favour of the device, bled dry
The bones of the Earth now a playground of ignorance and war
A timeless portrait of a battered broken land
Yet still the shadow of hope feathers its mark
Burning goodness remains, deafening in small pockets
The compass of charity and passion rages outward
The smell of love alive and strong, beating, beautiful
Beating back the evils of violation and fear
Our raw emotions lighten the way against the tainted darkness
An antidote to the stinging poison in us all
Suppressed by the lucky few, barely controlled and black
This though the seeds of life we endure
Deep and serious, shrivelled yet strong, black but white
Open arms ready with clenched fists
Attentive hearts with our backs turned
Stitched together with stone and button skin
The contradictions rage on infecting sanity and mind
Torn souls battered and confused by the end
An overdose of existence both damned and damning
And beyond way past the warm light
By our own demented arrogance, up or down we go
A reflection of who we touched and what we did
Good or bad, lost or found this is...this is...
The day we lived our life.

About the author

Hello.
I am not the author. I am merely the narrator.
You know the author. You have seen this person, worked with this person, laughed with this person, cried with this person.

Remember that person you bumped into at the shopping centre; that was the author.
Remember that person you drove past walking on the pavement; that was the author.
Remember that person sitting 3 rows in front of you in the cinema; that was the author.
Remember that person with the big fat colouring book; that was the author.
Remember that person you looked at and judged instantly without knowing the slightest thing about them; that was the author.

Remember your biggest regret in life; that was the author.

(there will be times when it is perfectly fine to stop reading this book and take a minute. in fact, this is one of those times. you have just read "about the author" and are probably sat, or stood, scratching your head thinking about the biggest regret in your life. we all have them. we all wonder about them and what could have been. me included. so take a minute...don't be so hard on yourself. don't suddenly come to the realisation that you only get one chance in life. remember, regret is just a word...just like love...and suicide...and the life in-between)
So, this is where it may get a bit complicated. Like I have said, I am not the author...merely the humble narrator. Which means I will be narrating the life of the author who is not actually writing this book in the sense that an author does; more acting and reliving it as I narrate it to you, the reader. Is everyone with me? Good.

(if I was you, I would re-read that last sentence...maybe a few times...you understand...good)

Then let's continue..."this heat, it's hell closing in on me".

Birth

Cracking and spitting, the violence,
this disguise of new life is ripped,
a metaphor for the end,
a scream of silence and freedom.

A twig snaps underfoot,
a carcass opens its eyes,
breathes a snow sunset
and flies on a wave of memory.

And so this beginning, this birth,
mere cement for a frail humanity,
moral support in a demoralised land,
a stage of cripple and wealth.

We cradle and burp a bastard sigh,
we congratulate suffering and disease,
and by cutting the single life cord,
we prove this metaphor for the end.

<u>Start</u>

(grab a coffee)

The thing is, Death does actually look exactly like what you imagine. Go on. Imagine what Death looks like...you got the picture in your head? Yeah? Well, it actually does look like that... who would have thought?! In just a few moments, our intrepid author is about to come close to Death for a second time in his short life.

(basically, the first time involved our baby author eating dog shit off the garden and spending a long time in hospital)

It was a day just like this one (**look out the window**) – that is if today is sunny and bright. Splish splash, splish splash, splish splash...this is the sound the other kids were making in the outdoor swimming pool. Fun was being had and laughs were being...er...laughed?! Smiles, joy; freedom. Our young author was on the outside looking in but most definitely wanted to get in despite not knowing how to swim. So, with a big run and jump... in he went, straight into the deep end!

The sharp chill of the water iced over the skin, its clasp around the unsuspecting body of this poor soul now fully submerged was tight and endless. Sudden panic sparked the helpless thrashing as water gorged down a twisted mouth silencing horrific screams of fear and mortality. Arms flailed and legs kicked, an almost peaceful realisation was setting in as time slowed to a crawl; a place among the stars was dawning free. Death stood at the pools edge, its prize not to be denied again when suddenly something ironic happened...

(the irony will be explained at a later stage in the authors life)

...a strong pair of arms plunged into the pool and in one brilliant motion, dragged the author out and onto the side coughing and spluttering. Everyone was staring motionless from the pool as our author slowly regained a steady breath, lungs now empty of the chlorine flavoured liquid. The strong arms that had made this rescue belonged to a dad. Not just anyone's dad mind...but the authors dad.

(from now on, I am gonna give the author a name. it will get very irritating if I keep referring to the author as "the author" or "our author" throughout. so, I will call our author...James. same name as me...easier to remember that way)

James felt the full air of life fill his entire being and Death was once again disappointed. Towering over him, Death engulfed James with a shadow shrieking in loss and pain and spoke, "You better get used to me being over your shoulder boy" and with that he vanished leaving James shivering with Death's shadow slowly seeping into his body.

End

A lone saxophone draws me awake and eases me into the land of the living. A soft whispering wall of background noise caresses my tired eyes allowing light to creep in. I begin to stretch my bones and muscles and feel my heart beat to the sound of rhythm bass; steady and strong. My breathing is calm and regular which just a very slight skip to it, accompanied by a foghorn of music that combines into one glorious chorus.

My soul is becoming bright and warm with every passing second, a rainbow of joy and complication with its own specific dance and sway; a click of the fingers, a shift of the hips. I stand tall and stiff reaching up to the very stars that adorn my surroundings and reach for one that is engulfed by flame and pulsating with energy; is this Eden? I jump high, I jump higher, I jump as high as I have ever done and I am off, floating towards this possibility of peace and desire.

I drift past the lost ones, the ones who need someone to live by; the rockers and the rollers. I see the young...no! I see the 'far too young to be here' with their painful expressions and forced smiles clawing their way upwards. I see them as they see themselves and it breaks my heart. I see the marks on their arms and the trail of tears they leave behind. Their soundtrack is one of string and organ, melancholy and sad but with a sharp bite that hits hard. Whatever led them here in life begins to peel away the skin they cling onto and a new one forms; divine and beautiful. And they sore with a purpose once missing, now reclaimed; god speed.

Then there are those who have given up on their merry way and now fall back down to Earth and beyond; deep into the depths of Hell. Not even wanting to scream as they flush past me, their very being completely content and lost with a random noise of thumping and cracking. I pity these poor souls, their inheritance of pain and suffering awaiting them is cruel and forever, a twisted take on the blues.

I break through and feel the heat of Eden as I fly and fly and fly. Whales rotate and loop the loop with a fixed grin keeping me safe and guiding my way. The cats that were drowned, the dogs that were beaten, the elephants whose tusks were taken away all look to me with a belief in a better place.

Flesh and bone have no power.

Material objects held so dear become meaningless.

Black and white merges into light.

And all the thoughts and experiences of suffering and pain melt away and become a divine strength of eternal happiness.

This is where people like me will go.
This is where the shadows cannot reach.
This is the spirit of Eden.

And then the beating begins. My self-destruct will never allow me to be at peace in this spirit of Eden and I begin to fall...fast, and hard. My plummet causes a screech grating my ears and piercing my eyes as I speed past the pigs; tumbling swine. They flap about and snort away their own lost opportunities reaching for me with their stupid little pink feet with a panicked realisation burning in their gaze.

The slices and scars on my arms and legs sting once again and an excitement washes over me in sharp breathes and small moments. I reach up to whence I have fallen from and scream at whatever God banishes me from his Eden coming to the only conclusion I can; God is dead and suffers in hell with the rest of us disturbed and broken souls. Blood flows free from my wounds and covers my body in a skin of pure red as I fall deeper past a march of suicides all locked in a loop of death and rebirth, death and rebirth. All lined up, all forced into a position to die by the cruelty and ignorance of humanity, it breaks my heart and angers my mind as one by one they topple.

I land, crumpled and twisted, the shadow of the ruined standing over me and grinning. How did he get so strong? How did he get so big? He reaches down and picks me up by the neck bringing me nose to nose with him and holds me fast. I feel his hand melt into my neck and my scream is horrible and loud. Our noses come together and merge as my violent kicking joins with his firm stance as bones crack and break. My screaming is drowned out as our faces collide, my body burns as red skin crashes against black shadow and our hearts explode into tiny pieces before reforming as one loud beat. His voice rings deafening in my mind and I learn the tragic truth of who he is and break down; this is becoming.

I stand alone in nothingness with a full realisation that this world has beaten me. I didn't want this. I didn't deserve this. Neither did my Mother. I now know everything. I now feel everything...it is time to be erased from this existence, time to be remembered as a coward, time to be added to the list of statistics amongst the broken.

A light appears from somewhere and I see the shadow once again; this beautiful liar...

(death burns in our breath. fears reside in our tears. there is no escape from our fate. and hand in hand we sway...together, tomorrow, today. James told me this once. told me of his despair in getting so close to Heaven but ultimately falling to Hell. sad really)

A ring binder full of empty dreams (or the blinking cursor on a blank screen) ((or just a bunch of dirty thoughts))

James sits staring at the computer screen. The pure brilliant white shines across features and frowns as brown eyes, deep and old, scan into empty space searching for inspiration and life. Strands of long dark hair droop across chubby cheeks and stick to an unkempt beard; wiry and itchy. Fingers hover over letters and keys...no ebb, no flow. His chest aches, his overweight belly rumbles and his calf muscle begins to cramp up.

He glances at the ring binder full of empty dreams. He stares at the four walls hemming him in. He sips at the boiling hot mug of coffee to his left. He plays with the smart scan mouse to his right. He does everything...except write.

(this is why, esteemed readers, I am doing the writing)
His concentration is beginning to fade.
His fingers find his phone.
His mind loses interest.
His time is now being wasted.
Inspiration is low.

There is a darkness

It dwells within us all.
It watches through our eyes.
It wanders down our halls.
It meets us in our shadow.

It messes with time.
It drives us insane.
It feeds the child in us.
It mutes the adult because of.

It maps out the wrong way.
It miss guides our compass.
It cages our bravery.
It reaches me lonesome.

There is a darkness.
That does dwell in us all.
But since when did darkness.
Ever snuff out the light.

The letter

NHS No: [redacted]

Tuesday, 08 October 2013

Private & Confidential

[redacted]

Dear [redacted]

RE: Counselling Appointment

An appointment for **counselling** has been made for you with a practitioner from the Primary Care Mental Health Team. Your appointment will take place on:

DATE: 8th October 2013

TIME: 9.00am

LOCATION: [redacted]

PRACTITIONER: [redacted]

Should this appointment be inconvenient please do not hesitate to contact the team on the above number to rearrange. Please report to reception on the ground floor when you arrive.

If you do not attend this appointment we will assume you no longer require counselling and we will discharge you back to the care of your GP.

Yours [redacted]

Counselling
Primary Care Mental Health Team

Cc GP:

Supporting Health and Wellbeing
Primary Care Mental Health Team

Useful contact numbers:
Mental Health Helpline: 0500 639 000; NHS Direct 0845 4647; The Samaritans: 0845 790 9090

Father and Mother

(we are not defined by our parents. our life is our own and the decisions we make are ours and ours alone. not so for James. sat in the counselling room, he thinks about his parents)

Father

I hear his demands, drunken and violent and see what he is doing to our family day in day out, bleeding us dry of any savings and only thinking of himself; my Father. Still to this day, his actions and presence continue to haunt me and this house.

I look at a certain room and remember my Mother making him a sandwich which was then thrown at her in anger. I walk past a certain step and look down to see myself huddled listening to arguments and shouting. I feel a certain door and touch the hole left by one of his many punches. I sit at a certain table and shudder from the smack across my young face. I make a certain meal and recall the verbal abuse for not cleaning the house. I hold a piggy bank he used to raid to feed his drinking urges, much more important than his kid's pocket money. I tighten a dripping tap and am saddened by the nights and nights of tears shed by my Mother. I stand in the centre of this house and have my senses bombarded by the pain and suffering held in these walls. I should have stood up to him more, I should have told him to get his shit together, I should have battered the badness out of him...I should have saved my Mother from this monster. But I didn't. He left and eventually my Mother died. What kind of son was I?! A useless piece of humanity that couldn't even save his own Mother; useless, worthless and pathetic. I will always hate myself that I did nothing. Until he was gone. After that, the only thing I did was to stop him from getting into this house with a kick to the stomach and by pinning him to the ground until 5 policemen came and took him away. But it was too late by then. The damage was well and truly done.

There was a weekend after he had gone that he came back and my Mother allowed him to stay, I think to try and work things out. I will never forget what he said to me, "I hope this happens to you". He actually wished that I would make his same mistakes and be in the position he was in. He actually wished that I would get married, constantly cheat on my wife, have 2 kids and become even more of a drunk than I would already be at this point. He wished that my wife would get Multiple Sclerosis and I would leave citing that to be the reason I left when in fact the real reason was that I ran off with a married woman. He wished that I would come crawling back for forgiveness after realising the terrible mistake I had made and be faced with a son who was not willing to forgive. "I hope this happens to you", words I will take to the grave, words that will never allow me to forgive this man, this husband, this Father.

Farewell

The last time I saw him was at the end of this weekend. I had to drop him off at this hostel place for people in his situation; no home, no family close, nowhere to go and no one who wanted him. It was a tiny room, very basic with a bunk bed and small table which housed a lamp and an alarm clock. And in that moment, for the briefest of seconds, when I walked him into this room there was a sliver of hope for me, a chance that I might not grow up to be like him; the way he wished it. I actually felt sorry for him. A wave of sadness crashed over me and it took all my strength and might to keep from crying. Even today, all these years later, when I think of that room that same feeling of sadness takes over.

Mother

I hear her kindness, soft and noble attempting to save our family day in day out, keeping our head above the rising water only thinking of us; my Mother. Still to this day, her actions and presence continue to hold onto me and this house.

I look at a certain room and remember my Father putting her down to which she rose higher. I walk past a certain step and look down to see myself comforted after all the arguments and shouting. I feel a certain door and touch the hole left by one of the many punches she managed to dodge. I sit at a certain table and know I am safe from more abuse, protected by her shield. I make a certain meal and recall the comments of thanks and moans of yum. I hold a piggy bank re-filled with extra pocket money to spend on penny sweets and jawbreakers. I tighten a dripping tap and am saddened by the nights and nights of tears shed by my Mother. I stand in the centre of this house and have my senses bombarded by the good memories and love held in these walls. I should have stood by her side more, I should have told her to get rid of him, I should have strengthened the goodness in her...I should have helped her defeat this monster. But I didn't. After all she had been through, she was left with a broken heart, lonely soul and decaying body. What kind of son was I?! A useless piece of humanity that couldn't even save his own Mother; useless, worthless and pathetic. I will always hate myself that I did nothing. Until he was gone. After that, I helped to look after her and support her through the constant appointments and many tests. Put my future on hold, get a job and share responsibility of the bills and debts. Take on all the things that come from having a 3 bedroom house and keeping it presentable and honourable. But it was too late by then. The damage was well and truly done

There was a weekend after he had gone that he came back and my Mother allowed him to stay, I think to try and work things out. I will never forget the feeling of utter disbelief and hurt I felt at my Mother's decision. After all he had done, not just recently but in the past, I was in shock that she would give him another chance. But then you realise that they had been married for years. You realise that despite all the shit he did, she loved him absolutely. You realise that as a nurse, my Mother knew exactly what was in store for her as a Multiple Sclerosis sufferer. You realise the enormous feeling of loneliness and pain ahead of you and come to the conclusion and question yourself...what would you do in that position?

Farewell

The last time I saw her alive was in the care home. We had been called backwards and forwards, day and night for the last month now expecting it to be the end. Today was to be the day. She was, and had been, unconscious for several days now. The disease had turned her into all skin and bones incapable of doing anything for herself, incapable of even forming words and sentences for us to understand and react to. Yet, even after her heart had been split in half, her soul left to wander alone and her body now its own enemy, I still remember she kept her smile and her uncompromising strength. In the end, her last breath was a mighty deafening roar and her final heartbeat was as strong and fast as a new born.

Father = **drunk'en** given to excessive drinking; worthless, besotted, resulting from intoxication. But we shouldn't just label James' Father as a drunken. He was so much more: liar, abusive, selfish, angry, dangerous, pathetic, scum **(you get the picture)**

Mother = **multiple sclerosis** a chronic progressive disease in which there is a patchy deterioration of the myelin forming a sheath for the nerve fibres, resulting in various forms of paralysis throughout the body. But we shouldn't just label James' Mother as a multiple sclerosis. She was so much more: loving, caring, protective, kind, innocent, helpful, warm **(a suffering angel)**

James = **lost** missing; not able to be found; thrown away, squandered; wasted, ruined. But we shouldn't just label James as a lost. He is so much more: suicidal, depressed, selfless, guardian, coward, brave, torn **(poor soul)**

(I think it is time you took a break. grab a cuppa. piece of cake or chocolate. fruit if you like? think about your parents. the influence they have had on you. a place among the stars)

Such a fool

Such a fool to believe, **(that he was free)**
such an idiot to feel, **(that he was loved)**
a few days saving grace **(from that voice)**
cannot change my place. **(never go away)**
That other side came back, **(was it always there?)**
that other side drew blood, **(the cutting started)**
more angry than before **(and dangerous)**
and ready for war. **(James – the battlefield)**
It is far too powerful, **(over)**
it is far too strong, **(hard)**
pain is a mean to an end **(James' end)**
a journey over my friend. **(no escape)**
And in this quiet room, **(with these four walls)**
and in this lonely box, **(mind)**
the shadow closes in **(seeping)**
bringing darkness within. **(no light)**
I was such a fool to think I could get through this, **(poor soul)**
I was such an idiot to feel any hope in my heart, **(poor man)**
those few days saving grace made me realise **(false)**
my place is surrounded by demons I cannot exorcise. **(part of him)**

(sometimes we sit together. just sit, no talking. we think about life, our place in the universe, the past, present and future. all the time wasted, all the opportunities missed. will we be remembered when we are gone? will the lives we have led be celebrated? will our names be spoken with admiration and respect? a distraction - the single piano note plays in the background, its striking sound echoes around these 4 walls. in this room, hearts have been poured out, tears have been shed, depression has been exposed. so clinical. so sterile. so hard)

Demons, demons everywhere. They live in us all. I can see James' demons. They stalk him constantly. Here he in front of this counsellor and they prance around him, smacking his face and whispering in his ear. They pull his hair and scratch his arms, spit in his face and piss in his eyes; one defecates in his mouth. They are at their strongest when he talks about his Father and at their weakest when he talks about his Mother.

James sits in the plastic chair picking his nails. His breathing is fast and his chest is heavy. He keeps crossing then uncrossing his legs, tapping his feet wildly and uncontrollably, clearing his croaky sounding throat. This fidgeting extends from head to toe and is at its worst in his mind.

"tick tock tick tock tick tock tick tock tick tock tick tock...fucking coward. why are you here? why are you talking to this fucking counsellor? she doesn't give a fucking shit...she gets paid to listen to you whine and bitch. boo fucking hoo. you think you can get rid of us? you really thing you can actually get rid of us! we are part of you...now and forever. there is no you without us...do you understand? there is no you without us. there is no you without us. there is no you without us. there is no you without us. there is no you without us. there is no fucking you without us!"

Our Place

Our place in history is written,
our mark well and truly made,
and just as one man's evolution,
is another man's religion,
we continue to strive forward,
we continue to live on.

And yet we are helpless,
powerless against mother nature,
and yet we are helpless,
victims from our own cruelty.
And yet we are brilliant,
our minds capable of much,
and yet we are brilliant,
our compassion capable of sacrifice.

Some say we are merely puppets,
some say we are barely a blip,
some say we should not be,
some say we cannot be.
But some say we are our own masters,
some say we are our own Gods,
some say we are own souls,
some say we are our own destiny.

Whatever we are,
we can be so much more,
whatever we are,
we can stop the cruelty,
whatever we are,
we can learn from our mistakes,
whatever we are,
we can secure our place.

We can secure our place? Where do we secure our place James wonders? Hell? Heaven? We spend so much time wasted and lost.

We look outwards when we should be looking inwards. We mask the hurt on the outside when we should be healing the inside. As James walks through the hospital, he passes wards and rooms full of life and reeking of death. Grieving families mix with celebrating fathers...two sides of the same coin, a joke with the same punch-line; our place in a world based on unpredictability and constant pain. And slowly we rot.

The lonely sound of a distant harmonica, a soundtrack to all the damaged goods out there, their exhausted notes a reminder of lost causes, their endless songs a warning to all that will follow. The divorcee desperate to capture lost youth. The abandoned bum desperate to capture lost change. The old drunk desperate to capture lost reasoning. The abused wife desperate to capture lost strength. The drug addict desperate to capture lost willpower. The stuck poet desperate to capture lost imagination. The serial cheat desperate to capture lost family. The street hooker desperate to capture lost respect. The cancer sufferer desperate to capture lost time. The suicide victim desperate to capture lost happiness. The struggling worker desperate to capture lost break. The orphaned child desperate to capture lost answers. The jail bird desperate to capture lost dignity.

The war veteren desperate to capture lost normality. The pregnant teen desperate to capture lost love. The suffering musician desperate to capture lost chords. The crying anorexic desperate to capture lost reflections. The broken heart desperate to capture lost pieces. The trapped mind desperate to capture lost freedom. The weathered pensioner desperate to capture lost breath. The lonely widow desperate to capture lost memories. The damaged goods desperate to capture lost recognition. And still the sound of a lonely distant harmonica plays on, a soundtrack to all the damaged goods in here, their exhausted symphony a reminder of lost charities, their endless collections an embracement to all that will follow.

(i am so lost. the space around me is so vast...it threatens to close in on me, wrap its hands around my throat and squeeze. the air

above me pulls me close and lifts my feet off the ground, floating away, sad, forgotten, desperate...lost; a spec of black in a meaningless life. who would remember? who would mourn? who would forgive? jagged nails. coffee breath. fat bastard. aching bones. talentless prick. just another statistic on a chalk board of formulas and lines. a day time television discussion in front of a packed audience salivating with hunger and staring with wild eyes...their appreciation summed up in a roar of laughter and mindless applause. hurrah for the freak, bravo for the pathetic, "more, more" for the joker, don't let him leave until we say so... his naivety the punchline. puncture his heart, piss on his kindness, revel in his innocence, kill his youth. no message from home for him...or me. no place amongst the stars for us. when the blackness comes, it comes hard. a chariot of fire and suffering will carry our souls through a bed of fog and ice, its contamination seeping into what we were and what we will become...coward...heathen... dust...ice...afraid of time, running away, a curled up carcass... into descent, into death, into dark; unto nothing...................
....)

James is falling. Tumbling into a deep black hole and frantically thrashing about, grasping thin air and hoping that it will grasp back. Specs of faint light catches his eye and draws on his attention. Faces appear from the darkness...flashes of features he recognises, a smile here, a wink there; he knows these people. Then he can see arms and hands flailing...no, not flailing, reaching...reaching out for him, wanting to save him and stop him from falling anymore. He sees their lips moving, hears words shouting at him "Stay!" they cry, "Don't leave us" they plead, "Help us" they scream. But he can't stay. He has to leave them. There is no help they can offer him. And so he keeps on falling...

What is the 9-5?

"It's a box, simple as that. It consists of restraints and rules, it demands you do not think outside of it, it can be as big or small as is dictated to you, it keeps you under control and caged in. Do not dare step outside of it. Do not dare try and break its 4 walls. Do not dare to try and beat it. Do not dare attempt to free yourself from it. Working a 9-5 job is like living in a zoo (although, animals don't actually *live* in a zoo really). You are told when to eat, what to do, how to act, rights and wrongs, ups and downs etc etc. I scan my identity into my job, my badge a barcode hanging around my neck. I have tasks I am meant to carry out on a daily basis...yes sir, no sir, please sir. I eat my food when I am told and take only as long as I am allowed. I am kept in my place and am punished if I step out of line or stop playing nice for the audience. I keep doing what I am doing so I can carry on living. But I am not living by carrying on what I am doing. So, why do I, or anyone else for that matter, keep on doing it?! ?!"

"My job is not of importance. I do not save lives or help those in need. I do not contribute to science or medicine. I do not create worlds or soundscapes. I do not build or craft. I do not progress or better myself. I do not live or die. I simply do and exist; limbo. My opinions do not matter. My health is of no importance. My personal life is to be separate. My very being is an oversight. My soul is worthless. My body is not my own. My mind is a complete waste of their time. My eye is..."

"And so we try to swim but sink. And so we try to breathe but suffocate. And so we try to run but fall. And so we try to speak but stutter. And so we try to fly but flap. And so we try to live but fail. And so we try to escape but fail. And so we try to reach but fail. And so we try to try but fail."

"What is the 9-5? It is everything we are not. It is the box we should never find ourselves in, the cage that should not hold us, the zoo that should not be. Since when did humanity become a slave to its own addiction and obsession with material goodies so much so that it is willing to sacrifice freedom and progression? Our evolution has come to a sad end as we indulge in the shit we hold so dear whilst our very creativity and wonder withers and dies. The fundamental purpose of life is lost through the numbers and pounds we strive to build upon and it is only in the precise moment of death that we realise what a horrible mistake we have made."

A crack in the ice

Amongst the angst of life and stone,
we struggle and question each decision,
our brave façade a crack in the ice,
our brave façade a false reality.

Surrounded by our hot water and bed linen,
comforted by the bricks that lock us in.
Proud of the fancy floors we walk upon,
our arrogance keeping us afloat any-ways.

The lure and pull of the cardboard office,
an excuse to ignore the family life.
The higher we climb up the corporate ladder,
a reason to look down on the empty spaces.

The fancy car, the crazy nights, the young lust,
the wife left at home nothing more than scum.
Kids, mere objects that get in the way,
their tears twisted, their blame reversed.

And as we pretend it's alright,
we pretend we can change.
And as we pretend it's normal,
we pretend we can stop.

Then before you know it, it's too late,
your past a sludge of unimportance,
your future limited to piss and wine,
and that crack in the ice now a hole.

At arms length

See that line pissed on the floor,
don't cross it, don't look at it.
See that barrier staring from my eyes,
don't question it, don't point at it.
See that silence coming from my mouth,
don't answer it, don't reach at it.

At arms length I stay,
at arms length I live,
at arms length I breath,
at arms length I am.

See that empty space I occupy,
don't fill it, don't dress at it.
See that hatred filling the air,
don't purify it, don't pity at it.
See that death over my shoulder,
don't bother it, don't forgive at it.

At arms length I wait,
at arms length I run,
at arms length I lust,
at arms length I die.

Breath

Trapped inside this faceless shell,
my true being hidden and hurt,
saddened and naked travelled and weary,
a freedom desired, a reality lost.

Why do we shiver and cower,
our self-loathing evident and on show,
freaks screaming in silence,
bleeding emotions empty and vanish.

Better to please boxed strangers,
burn our own paper bridges,
and ground the suicidal souls,
destined to meet again.

But all they say is 'that's life',
a sick twisted joke already written,
its punch line forever sought,
trapped inside this faceless shell.

Staring at the mirror, James watches the faceless shell have no reaction as he slices his arm again and again and again. How did it come to this? How did he end up doing this? He was strong. He got through a horrible part of his life. He has nothing to be sad about, nothing to complain over, and nothing that should make him do what he is doing again and again and again...and yet, he still does it.

The first time he did it was purely out of curiosity. What does it feel like? How deep could he go? How long could he get away with it before anyone notices? He did it in the bath to begin with, then it was over the sink, but, eventually, he just had a blade in his desk drawer and did it whenever he wanted. He could feel the skin being parted. See the blood escape and trickle. Sense the sharp pain and slight itch. Taste the mix of sweetness and iron. His arm looked like a cats scratching post. But it wasn't just the slices and cuts, there was also the damage done which couldn't easily be seen. The slapping and punching to his face and the biting to his "good arm".

Then there was the absolute lack of sleep and the dreams that taunted him when he did sleep. The feeling that the 4 walls that housed him for 36 years were closing in around him and squeezing the very fight out of him. The shitty neighbours that lived on either side. The lack of worth in his job. The absence of intimacy. The lonely feelings. The lost cause.

(people reading this are probably wondering how someone could hurt themselves. wondering how someone could cut their own arm on purpose and watch the blood trickle free. the pure harsh reality is simple...you could never know how or why someone would do this unless you are doing it yourself. you can only know if you are in that place reserved for those who have been pushed too far) (why can't things just be simple...those simple things)

In this overcomplicated world of man, method and madness, it's those simple things that shine and smile upon a frowning rainbow.

The cool breeze on a hot day, the click click of a writing pen, the noisy stiffness of a new book, the eureka moment of a lost memory, the warm feeling of freshly clean sheets, the scratch strike of a burning match, the sods law of a surprise thunderstorm, the joint glance from two would be lovers, the familiar beat of a deep bass drum, the unplanned ring of a welcome phone call, the sweet smell of a just cut lawn, the excited feeling of a snowy Christmas morning, the ivory tinkle of a grand piano sound, the deep purr of a well fed cat, the red light of a stand by button, the weird bend of a flexi ruler, the uneasy chill of a dark wood, the excitement felt from a quick kiss, the sudden emotion from an old photo, the time wasted from doing nothing.

And so, all these simple things, exist in a overcomplicated world, to bring that much needed balance, upon a frowning rainbow.

(who's talking now? is it James or is it me...the author. who is who? what is what? when is when? **James has been pushed to the absolute limits of existence** and life itself. pushed to the edge of the cliff **tip toeing his way over and into the abyss** but hanging on with everything he has left. and so, as we began, death does actually **look exactly like what you imagine**) Go on. Imagine what Death looks like...you got the picture in your head? Yeah? Well, it actually does look like that...who would have thought?! In **just** a **few** moments, our intrepid author is about to come **close** to **Death** for a third time**...me...me...me...me...me...me...me...me/james/ james/me/me/james/me...the same.)**

This is...

Visions of an end to signal a whole new beginning
Thrust from without, cries shear a heart attack
Tears that almost stave off death itself
This game over, these empty pockets
As rules that once bent now stiffen
And the limitations of humanity are boxed, a sadist
This reality of mortality a cruel reveal
Amongst a land of mud and stone
The bible of life replaced with the guide to death
A guide that guards the graveyard of past privelages
As decay swamps over anything once living and breathing
Eaten from the inside out, outlining remains
Horizons of what we once were now memories of colour
The bones of the soul now a matter of let it be
A timeless portrait of a darkness we fear
Yet still the shadow of hope feathers its mark
A burning belief in a living beyond
The compass leading those who choose to be led
The smell of black alive and strong, beating, beautiful
Beautiful like the fading photographs we leave behind
Our raw emotions clinging to those same pictures
An antidote to the stinging reality in us all
Our opeth now left with fragile minds
This through the seeds of death we must endure
Deep and serious, shrivelled yet strong, black but white
The boatmans arms ready with clenched fists
To take us on a trip over smothering water
Stitched together with stone and button skin
The conflictions rage through like scripted tears
Torn souls battered and confused by this beginning
An overdose of existence damned or saved
And led to the light we have chosen
By our own demented way, up or down we go
A reflection of who we touched and what we did
Good or bad, lost or found this is...this is...
The day death came to visit.

What Is Death?

A dance macabre, a haunted symphony,
what is death? who is death? where is death?

To some, the blackness is enough,
its cruel grip chokes the innocent
and blinds the young; yet death
does not discriminate,
nor does it choose,
the innocent, the guilty,
the young, the old,
all will face death...

...death; hooded?
Bony fingers wrapped around a splintered scythe?
Or merely a familiar grin; a familiar voice,
a familiar stare, a familiar love.
(Cause of death equals a broken heart.)
An action, a series of events, a coincidence?
A lack of discipline. A life wasted.

Its weight a constant burden,
its breath a constant cloud,
its presence a constant worry.

And yet this fear of death keeps us alive,
whispers sanity when insanity nags,
stops us when we need to be stopped,
gives us strength when we are weak,

but death...

...also takes away those we care about
and makes us hate it, despise it, loath it,
and question it...

Death is many things.

I believe death is lonely
and when my time comes,
I would consider it an honour
to accompany it
and to embrace it
and to consider it...
...my friend - death.

We all die

And so it will come to us all,
from the moment we are born
this inevitability awaits,
with patience and grit.

The importance will come,
from not how or when,
but what we leave behind
and where we will go.

Independent beliefs,
desired religions,
worshipped Gods,
feared Demons.

We all die,
sooner or later.

We all die,
younger or older.

We all die,
man or woman.

And so it will come to us all,
I do not fear my friend – death,
this journey awaits,
with open arms and inevitability.

Now

A bruised thunderous sky,
as clouds erupt with tears,
and the sweet smell of emotion,
cleanses a devastated world,
what once was a forest of colour,
is now a graveyard of stump,
what once was a monsoon of life,
is now an infinity of death.

Moonlight casts over skeletons shadows,
an eerie torment forever etched,
as even now they huddle together,
always running from this inescapable fate.

The Earth grumbles and licks its wounds,
scared forever diseased by ignorance,
a scorched land bleeds and scabs over,
it's daily cycle limps on, this trapped ghost.

Hellish lightning slices through thick air,
barren sands eat away forgotten achievements,
and the ruins of a lost way of life weep,
as an uncontrollable sadness laps broken borders.

A piercing sun breaks through black skies,
forcing even death to scramble for the shade,
as oceans begin to boil and grounds begin to crack,
the blinding rays splitting open all it touches.

This distant planet once proud and blue,
now a charcoal shell of deconstruction and loss,
begins its long creep into blind nothingness,
howling as it goes, a pinprick through dead space.

When beauty dies

A sultry sway,
a sexy tilt.

Daring whispers
slay the night,
bring dark eyes
lord of light.

A slender neck,
curves of sex.

That innocent way.

But a broken heart.
But an abused body.
But a shattered mind.
But a battered soul.

When beauty dies,
death's cold touch
now a warm shoulder,
helps on as such.

Is the gentleman,
is the lost love.

Death the sonnet,
death the brave,
death the guide,
death the save.

The Death Of Music

And so, in the distance, a record player crackles,
its RPM slowing down to a cruel wheezing plod,
and just as the art of live music drowns its own corpse,
the cresendo builds to play the death of music.

The skill of the instrument now a frowned upon memory,
tacky backing tracks partner with cold electronica,
and the writer is reduced to a forgotten matter of fact,
lyrics no more than a collection of empty obedience.

Rushing waves of talentless copycats storm the stage,
originality long gone and vanished by a brash sweep,
as we churn out puppets happy to sing by their strings,
our crash test dummies content to be taken for the ride.

And so, the true greats,
they turn in their graves,
their souls weep with despair,
their achievements diluted and lost,
the foundation they built gone,
a forgotten pile of old rubble,
battered and broken...

...picked through by the select few,
kept alive by the different,
and shared amongst the believers,
who learn the meaning of music,
and give body to it's ghost,
ensuring the death of music,
is merely it's encore.

Pain

Suffocating with pain.

This death brings
loneliness and blood,
a thick fear of the end,
a thick fear of the black.

Terrified, gasping,
every breath precious,
every beat hard,
every second deep.

Grinning with pain.

Beyond mere feeling,
nerves of chains,
a blank coldness sets in
and whispers a lullaby.

Reaching, wishing,
that final release of life,
that final clenched fist,
that final burnt image.

Walking with pain.
Lost with pain.
Gone with pain.

My Nurse

My nurse was my mum,
her kindness bright,
her soul strong.
My nurse was my mum,
her teachings honoured,
her students blessed.
My nurse was my mum,
her future ahead,
her hospital home.

My nurse was my mum,
her eyes failing,
her body weak.
My nurse was my mum,
her legs supported,
her energy low.
My nurse was my mum,
her future wavering,
her hospital fading.

My nurse was my mum,
her hope vanished,
her mind hurting.
My nurse was my mum,
her nerves shattering,
her clock slowing.
My nurse was my mum,
her future limited,
her hospital distant.

My nurse was my mum,
her life remembered.

The Wall

Can you see the patterns on the wall?
the scratches carved by broken fingers,
the warnings left by worn down bone,
the evidence of death's numb hunt.

Can you see the screams in the wall?
screams of ignored pleas,
pleas of pathetic loss,
loss of a wasted life.

Can you see the look from the wall?
eyes of longing disappointment,
eyes of stern inevitability,
eyes of a blank cold brick.

Can you see the hell beyond the wall?
the home of your peers,
the eternity you deserve,
the conclusion of death's numb hunt.

Nowhere to hide

The midnight dawn,
the dark sockets,
death's cold grin,
nowhere to hide.

This forever night,
this weeping truth,
a certain outcome,
nowhere to hide.

And a beauty noise,
shines the only path,
ticks the tock,
nowhere to hide.

Lost footprints crack,
a fallen soul gone,
those left behind,
nowhere to hide.

The daylight breaks,
the innocent sight,
life's warm wink,
nowhere to hide.

Arc

A swamped with a low hum; it breathes,
soars beyond our sonic understanding,
climbs above material restrictions and logic,
and covers with a wave of collapse and infinity.

The tick cancels the tock; it ends,
numbers waltz into a universe of peace,
their meaning free and set in flight,
burning through a dark cosmic absolution.

Passing over concrete and stone; we fly,
our minds glee causes stars to grin,
the glass reflection shattering with light,
showering the blackness with a torrent of life.

And a distant choir guides us; our fate,
riding the conductors lunatic symphony,
to a destination visited only in lost dreams,
a world shaped by our honesty and hopes.

Surrounded by our insides out; our deconstruction,
the swaying flowers of imagination bloom,
and a very special arc crashes against the horizon,
the rainbow bridge glimmering in the distance.

This is the life after the death; it breathes,
welcoming with smiles and laughter,
those thought lost embrace with open arms,
a swamped with that low hum.

A dieing man

Alone in this cold house, bare and tired I sit,
aware of time, aware of a fading heartbeat;
I laugh and scream and breath.

I am not afraid any more, my work is done.
(the importance of money now trivial)

The tick tock of distant clocks,
bring me closer to death,
this soundtrack of memory and loss,
a sweet sonnet of the everyman,
on a fading photograph of my world,
once full of colour and sound...

...now echoes are all that remain,
mortality gathers like powder,
and a saxaphone plays in the night,
the insanity of existence tilts its head,
my eyes begin to weep and blur.

I am prepared, I am saddened, I am ready.
I remember games,
I remember grass,
I remember words,
I remember the key.

And all that I am,
and all that I was,
all that I did,
all that I learnt,
all that I loved,
all that I hated,
and all that I could have been,
it all comes to an end,
a final smile,
a final breath
a final tick tock.

Sing

And on your last breath,
and on your final grasp,
and on your remaining beat,
and on your fixed stare...

...a distant song draws you away,
a distant sight catches your eye,
a distant reach pulls you closer,
a distant voice calls you on...

...you glance back once more,
you miss those you leave behind,
you feel their despair,
you know you will see them again...

...the light surrounds your soul,
the infinity completes your journey,
the day has only just begun,
the song only just to be sang.

Sublime

Heavy eyes glaze over and finally succumb,
a lasting beat echoes from a tired heart,
and a sublime silence hangs in the air.

Coldness collapses across tired skin,
now nothing more than an empty shell,
its occupant free of life's pretty asylum.

Time's void sets in stone a sombre hum,
this shift in tone thick and sweet,
a kaleidoscope of charcoal emotions.

And death welcomes a new friend,
a wild odyssey of belief begins,
odd times...and all.

A Drift

A freedom, you and me, a drift,
a sometime feeling of just let it be,
everyday troubles evaporate,
gorged upon by the moonlight,
absorbed by the fountain of stars
and lost amongst the dark strawberry sky.

And off we go, you and me, a drift,
our lives now empty spaces,
our history far behind us,
and hand in hand through death,
welcomed by the lovers and the saints
and found amongst the cool brilliant sky.

Looking back, you and me, a drift,
smiling at our rights and wrongs,
our long game complete,
our winning prize; each other,
together by the pearly white gates
and forever amongst the blue heavenly sky.

The Boatman Waits

Shadowless, eyeless...the boatman waits,
a patient tap on the shoulder,
a crack of bone a close distant,
a gentle reminder of time left.

Flip a coin, payment in full...the boatman waits,
atop this transport for one,
atop this ship made of passage,
atop this sea full of mud.

Neither good, nor evil...the boatman waits,
no judgement made by its hand,
no discrimination made by its head,
no destination made by its choice.

Forever, constant...the boatman waits,
you decide how you meet,
you decide how it looks,
you decide how...and where it takes you.

The Death of Death

Stars blazed and screamed,
black holes crushed; consumed,
the universe was ripping apart,
and an end was coming.

Death drifted amongst the violent silence,
a helpless witness sombre and alone.
As blind fires raged and blistered the dark,
inferno's of pain ripped apart worlds and suns.

Tornados of rock exploded,
the coldness of space boiled,
at once all empty spaces converged
imploding to a minus nothingness.

And for a moment, death was everything and everyone,
just as everything and everyone was death...

...this wasn't just the end,
this was the death of death.

2013...2013...END...

Part Two

31st December
Farewell

A reflection of a year,
memories of pain and hurt,
and visions of scars and blood,
farewell to two zero one three.

I remember the torment,
I see the echoes of cutting,
I hear the demon inside my head,
and listen to its forked tongue.

A loneliness smothered my being,
darkness my only company,
bitterness my only taste,
a coldness my only feeling.

Then came tablets,
then came counselling,
then came understanding,
then came freedom.

And now a new year beckons,
a fresh start or a diseased continuation?
only the passage of time will tell,
only the passage of time will be.

1st January
Success

In the last hours of 2013,
came a phone call number unknown,
and after a voicemail left,
came a very welcome success.

Third in a self-publishing comp,
bringing a genuine smile to my face,
something actually went my way,
signalling a fresh start this very day.

It is possible to do anything,
as long as you believe,
it is possible to live your dreams,
a worthwhile life it seems.

So here I am finally ready,
to take on the world and win,
bring light into my every present darkness,
no longer wandering in blind aimlessness.

In third place is **Love Or Suicide And The life In Between** by **James S M Parker**. An incredibly powerful and moving book that portrays the author's raw emotion as he travels through a particularly dark period of his life. You feel **James**' heavy mood and pain. The 'Useful Quotes' I found particularly poignant.

A very brave book to write, brilliantly written.

The 'Introduction' and the 'Thanks' also deserve a mention, they help you feel even closer to the author.

The layout, grammar and cover of this book are excellent too and I sincerely hope that **James S M Parker** continues to write as he most definitely has talent!

Very lovely to see that all profits will be donated to **The Samaritans**.

2nd January
Drag my carcass

Suddenly my carcass is dragged from sleep,
thrown under a shower of pain and disdain,
scrubbed clean then forced to wear the uniform,
an embodiment of the masters deform.

Passing the other lost souls through window coldness,
a journey and location of swift predictability,
I now become the drone expected of me,
and take my place amongst the ghastly.

Where is the joy, where is the meaning?
An eight hour day of thick sludge and pointless bickering,
culminating in a sad realisation in mind
of the blind bleeding the blind.

And then my prayers for release are answered,
freedom for now as I drag my carcass,
way back home allowing myself a tiny smirk,
for that was the first day back in work.

3rd January
All with my…

I went into work today,
I spoke to my fellow colleagues,
I checked some parts off,
I drank some coffee.

I went to the post office on dinner,
I sent out my #FF's on Twitter,
I finished checking parts off,
I ate some chocolate.

I stopped Aga from getting a warning,
I laughed a bit, smiled a bit,
I finished work early,
I then went to the supermarket.

I picked up a card and cake,
I picked up bin bags and cat food,
I picked up non-alcohol wine, yum,
I drove home swiftly.

I surprised my girlfriend,
wished her a Happy Birthday,
gave her gifts and card (cake comes later),
I turned up the heating.

I ran my bath and hid the cake,
I checked all my emails and undressed,
I then realised that I did all the above,
all with my boxer shorts on inside out.

4th January
Escape

I close my eyes and imagine a freedom,
an escape from the grime and shit,
a release from all the trappings,
an end to smothered normality.

This asylum of ignorance and swine,
inmates shuffling along, this walking dead,
with heads down and shoulders slumped,
no respect for each other's pathetic existence.

They rip and shred their fellow kin,
beat and burn any wayward glance,
pillage the very land they live on
and waste away the precious time given.

To hell with thy neighbour,
let's snarl at the homeless man,
why *don't* we poison our bodies?
And corrupt our brains.

Our maker must truly despair in silence,
sob and wonder where it all went so wrong,
pray for someone to answer *their* prayers,
get to the punch line of this sick joke.

I open my eyes and see a prison,
a planet full of grime and shit,
no release from all the trappings,
no end to this smothered normality.

(well - there is one release)

5th January
I creak...

I creak...
and I ache.
I tire...
and I weaken.
I frown...
and I crease.
I swallow...
and I drown.
I freeze...
and I stiffen.
I sleep...
and I disturb.
I cough...
and I wheeze.
I see...
and I cry.
I work...
and I despair.
I hurt...
and I ignore.
I touch...
and I soften.
I create...
and I destroy.
I sweet...
and I sour.
I welcome...
and I collapse.
I hope...
and I darken.
I remember...
and I regret.
I live...
and I die.

6th January
Dreams

A marching band leads us on
into a universe of possibilities,
a kaleidoscope of dreams
and endless living stories
written with flight in mind,
immortality a given
and superpowers a must.

Grant me a beautiful landscape
to call my very own,
mould into shape at will
and bend to my needs and desires
through grace and determination,
am I a God
or merely a child?

And when the clouds turn dark
and our imagination births demons,
a pit of repressed pain
manifested in vivid detail
and horrific actions,
dragging our souls to the very edge
of our own personal hell.

We tumble through the worlds
created by the spark inside,
glorious and deadly
good vs evil
up and down,
it's our very own escape of need
from a reality of limitations...

...called life.

7th January
Head down...

Head down...keep going.
Head down...focus on the job.
Head down...plan ahead.
Head down...stick to the plan.
Head down...understand the task.
Head down...earn the pay.
Head down...take it on the chin.
Head down...learn from mistakes.
Head down...keep calm.
Head down...stay organised.
Head down...drink coffee.
Head down...time is your friend.
Head down...remember to breath.
Head down...shut up 'n play your guitar.

8th January
The scars

I can still feel the ridges,
now a darker shade of pink
etched into pure skin,
a thousand words
forever telling their story,
forever locked in pain,
forever a reminder.

Some deep, some faint,
their journey delicate at first,
occasional footsteps barely visible
until despair took over,
turned them into giant leaps,
gave them a silent voice
of tears in blood.

Now they travel with me,
from the inside to the out,
a sideways glance churns away,
and sends me right back to that place,
right back to that time,
and a demon inside disturbs,
a demon inside awakens.

9th January
Limp...

Limp...
drained, breath
bring me light,
a one night stand,
a desire,
bitter and joy
a bath of sweat,
fuck me hard,
blinking in utter...
...astonishment
and crazed blood,
a joined darkness
swaying amongst
stars in ink,
so deep,
so thick,
mirrored sex
our mouths collide
and melt,
stretched out and fucked...

...a passion, it lingers and sings,
connecting and transcending
taking with it all rational thought
and infusing together heart and soul
for that perfect moment that hangs...

...and hangs.

10th January
Untitled

Don't you just want to rip this whole fucking world apart?
Bring it to its knees and kick it when it's down.
Burn it to a crisp and then piss all over the ashes.
Be rid of humanity and its fucking arrogance.

So much suffering.
So much pain.
So much ignorance.
So much war.
So much death.

Man destroys man.
Country fights country.
Religion is a stigmata of religion.
This land of rape and honey.
Pathetic.

If there truly was the one maker,
imagine his/her disappointment,
imagine his/her embarrassment,
imagine his/her anger,
imagine his/her tears.

The human race is not a race; barely even human.
We are bullies, and animals, and pigs.
Our miraculous minds wasted.
Our wondrous Earth aborted.
Damn us all to Hell.

11th January
The apple tree

Under a bridge,
on the side of a road,
is an apple tree.

Bright and fruitful,
it spills its spoils,
for all to see.

Yet no one stops,
and no one picks,
even though it's free.

So please shed a tear,
from the side of the road,
for this lonely apple tree.

12th January
Transcend – part 1

The cannibalistic nature of life,
a writhing swarm of beetles and ants
carrying us through oil and dead skin,
a decomposing mess of shit and piss.

The sharp edges of the truth,
reflected with disdain and sadness
by the bottom of an empty glass,
a shattered realisation of waste and talent.

Sing with me a chorus of sorrow,
our last hurrah of half-hearted defiance
before our tongues are ripped out,
tossed to the dogs as mere appetisers.

And as our souls crumble and break,
any time we had abruptly ends,
not with a whimper, not with a bang,
but with a single tear over bone and teeth.

13th January
Sorrow

There are times when I wander through a place not of this place but a dark place. Its landscape covered with thick sludge with an aroma of treacle in the cold air. Clouds of black crows dripping with oil circle above whilst mountains impose and claw their way across the horizon. Red eyes watch and blink from every space and crack; burning with desire and hatred, their gaze brings drowsiness and fear.

I am forever urging my body to go forward in the sticky dead ground but am continuously forced backwards towards a truth I do not wish to uncover. I think I see figures in the blinding wind; shadows of enormous colossi stalking this sorrowful land and I begin to question my own sanity. Is this hell? Or is this reality? Have I been forsaken to my own inferno? Or is this merely a dream of sorts?

And as before, I cannot say for sure what existence this is. I stand still on a path, assigned, it seems, to me and me alone. A flickering dying light in a swarming breathless blackness; awash with shit and piss, I am fading...fading...fading. And as my eyes falter, this dark place becomes me. It pumps through my veins and fills my lungs. It deafens my ears and cages my heart. It seeps into my bones and rips apart my mind. And finally, with a thunderous mighty noise, earth splitting and painfully sharp; my soul cracks.

Time stops. Cruel clarity bestows upon my final thought and the truth is revealed................and then lost, leaving behind a sorrow...and a single tear.

14th January
Addicted

A need for more,
impulse,
give me give me.
Rational thought?
Addictions overcome any,
the desire is to great,
painfully,
twisting sanity,
distorting time,
this jilted poison,
the relief,
an orgasm of
a personal vice.
Then comes the high.
To hell with consequence,
who cares about the hurt,
addicted to the itch,
addicted to the scratch,
addicted to the rinse and repeat.

15th January words

hatred
desire
false
death
knowledge
power
revenge
watching
loneliness
murder
time
sorrow
pain
ignorance
scab
forgotten
joy
fun
despair
space
replace
build
destroy
create
drown
bound
bleed
nothing
puppet
love
suicide
life
words.

16th January
a fool...part 1

I give up...you have won.
I am the fool you knew I was,
the corruption of the good,
the failure of the brave.

The darkness fills my sight,
any light now a mere fantasy,
a cruel beacon that once was nothing,
nothing but a punishment of hope.

My head droops with fatigue
for too long have I fought,
too long have I wished for,
too long have I dreamt.

I should never have strived to be better,
I should never have believed in myself,
I should never have trusted those around me,
I should never have opened my heart.

I am pathetic, I am pitiful,
I have no home, I have no place,
I deserve this, I deserve everything,
I will burn, I will suffer.

And so my judgement has been made,
my destiny decided and executed,
a sentence of eternal suffering and blackness,
reflected by the sliver of a blade...

...the way it was always meant to be.
A fool in a room with a smile,
knowing and content,
fallen from the greatest of all heights.

17th January
Dust

Amongst the dead skin.

In a dark corner.

A mind cradled.

A body smashed.

Rocking in silence.

Out of reach...forever.

18th January
...a slave

To take a man's freedom,
is to take his very existence.

To destroy a man's pride,
is to sentence him to death.

To whip him till he bleeds,
is to scar his very soul.

To spit on his face,
is to embarrass his might.

To work him to the bone,
is to break his defiance.

To feed him leftover scraps,
is to starve his resolve.

To string him up by his neck,
is to suffocate his mind.

To have him call you master,
is to stifle his words.

To take away his identity,
is to turn him into a puppet.

To make a man a slave,
is to condemn you to hell...

...and...

...to think this still goes on,
is to lose faith in humanity.

19th January
COFFEE

Cups and cups of the stuff
Oh so sweet and dark
First thing in the morning
Fresh and steaming
Especially in the winter
Especially in bed

20th January
Swim

How'd you start a story in this world today?
How'd you even imagine the young man's waltz
and the middle age shuffle, the cream of the crop,
a mass of huddled humanity remembering lost days,
dirty women, sweet nicotine and cheap booze...
...I wanna fly away and look down from above,
imagining that it ain't all that bad all the time;
who you trying convince, me...or you?

Were you ever a coward? A sucker in the corner?
Damned if you do, doubly damned if you don't,
bet that view from above knocks you down a peg?
Hurts like a bastard when you come a calling,
drowning in parents "*told you so*" and "*amount to nothing...*"
...fuck them, fuck you, fuck the MAN, fuck the world,
that's the spirit boy, a whoop and a high five;
coming from a cough and a gutter.

And you swim like a torch fading from a dead battery,
flickering with the end of a great mighty adventure,
a falsehood told to boost lost pride and shrivelled up balls,
you did this, you did that, you were there, you lived,
bullshit! You survived and existed and sucked doin it...
...but don't we all? Fucking limited by our own passions,
boxed in by our own fears and beginnings;
something we only get and regret at the end.

21st January
p pii CK aWayyyy

I wwwannnnaaaa……

cleave ((((ccllllllEEEE aave) YOuR

FUCKING FUCKING FUCKING…

…face in.

p pii CK aWayyyy

AT YOuR brAiNssssssssssss –

www aLL oww

IINNNNN

YOuR

bbbbbbllllllloooooodddddddd…………….

and then simply do the tango with your butchered corpse.

22nd January
a blank space

Sometimes I just stare.

23rd January
Dunno?!

I am at a loss today,
as to what I write.
Staring at a white wall
doesn't really help.
Moving my head around
just brings boredom.
I pick at my nails,
nothing comes of it.
Even the cup of coffee
denies any inspiration.

Handling various objects
and stroking my stubble.
Scratching my back
and tapping my feet.
Fingering the mouse
and stroking the keyboard.

I am still at a loss,
as to what I write.
Not even Joy Division
can give any insight.
The dreaded writers block,
what a complete bastard.
Suppose my mind is blank,
can't be bursting every day.
Happens to the best of us,
happens to the worst.

24th January
What am I?

What am I?
Why am I?
Who am I?
Where am I?

Staring at a cracked reflection,
thirty six years staring back,
a look of hatred and inspiration,
a look of pitiful waste.

I see a face covered in loss,
colour faded through dry tears,
eyes that shimmer with rage
and a forced smile that quivers.

Am I something in that mirrored world?
A force of fucking nature,
someone who is respected and feared,
someone who is strong and tall.

The air flickers, impossibility smashed,
where exactly am I?
Alive or dead, good or bad?
Here...or there?

Where are those roads untraveled?
Please let me go, please just let me go.
Standing still on a highway of dust,
an echo of a light that never comes.

And behind me is what's in front of me,
this torture of a scarred existence,
an emptiness of unanswered pleas,
an emptiness of unwanted pain.

And why am I?
Who is responsible for this me?
It's a joke...right? A big laugh,
a big fucking laugh.

Funny, because we are not laughing,
my cracked reflection sharing my opinion,
one thought from one mind
to burn it all the fuck down.

I am nothing!
I mean nothing!
I am no one!
I am nowhere!

25th January
Sometimes

Sometimes I just want to be left alone.

Sometimes I don't want to talk.

Sometimes the darkness comforts me.

Sometimes being alone does me good.

Sometimes I don't feel like smiling.

Sometimes hating is better than liking.

Sometimes pain is better than pleasure.

Sometimes feeling down is preferable to up.

Sometimes caring is overrated.

Sometimes I am not interested in anything.

Sometimes giving up is easier than fighting.

Sometimes attack is better than defence.

Sometimes broken can never be fixed.

Sometimes dreaming beats reality.

Sometimes the ending can't come quick enough.

Sometimes wrong is better than right.

Sometimes I wish you would just fuck off.

Sometimes death is more appealing than life.

26th January
Explore…part 1

Softly, but with purpose and guidance, I lay you down,
staring into your blazing eyes I stretch your arms up high,
your naked body hums and beats with a wanting anticipation
as I run my hands over open palms and exposed wrists;
tonight my only desire is to explore
your very being…inside and out.

I hover my face over your neck,
breathing hot and heavy and hard.
Clawing my fingers down to your chest
I stop and feel your heart quicken
letting agonising minutes pass before I start to kiss your throat,
your head now angled upwards and rotating with slow motions
as I lower my hands and take in your perfect round breasts.

With slight careful movements, my strong digits caress and play,
my wet tongue now flicking over nipples sensitive and erect
while teeth send shocks pulsating with the slightest of nibbles
to the tips of your toes squirming and pointing downwards,
a sign that your body is aching for so much more pleasure.

My thumbs now mould over your
ribs and down your side stomach lines,
following the centre channel towards
your outstretched belly button
my tongue leaves a trail of passion and
coolness within your very core.
I pause and pull back glancing upwards
with a look of pure heat
before diving into the gorgeous hole
with furious devouring kisses.

27th January
I am going to Hell

And with my final breath hells womb swallows me up,
my soul plummeting fast and hard; dissection begins.
Castration, a frenzied feed takes away my manhood,
raped with barbed wire that tears my insides out.
Meat hooks claw my skin off exposing putrid flesh,
rotten by the many sins both fantasied and actioned.
Fire scalps my head and boils my screaming eyes,
what remains of my guts are vomited through my nostrils.
Minions rip out my nails and cut out my tongue,
my bones smashing as they hit rock bottom.
Now a mere puppet and plaything, I am lifted to my feet,
before me the demons salivating for amputation.
A butchering takes place, pain beyond description,
my corpse re-assembled and taken apart for eternity.

I deserve all I get.
I get what I deserve.

We are our own judge, jury and executioner.
We are our own enemy, our own punishment.
We are our own death.

28th January
Future isolation

Yesterday's today brings further isolation,
closer into a shell, closer into a wall,
after a sniff I want to cut again,
this drug of pain and colour; scarred.

My eyes dead with a misty coat,
seeing but not seeing, murky glaze,
a cold touch from a distant reach,
no comfort from these weak arms.

These words crawl into tomorrow,
a mind lost in time and despair
broken beyond any repair,
disdained from any absolution.

I am so tired.
Forgiveness not so.
I should...and will...burn in hell.

(written in the past about the future)

29th January
fresh scars

More red lines
over healed skin,
the twinge of pain
sliced with relief,
darkness clouds,
darkness rises,
darkness cuts.

Bleed with me,
give me release
from this shit,
like clockwork,
hatred builds,
hatred swims,
hatred cuts.

Burning cold eyes,
a lost stare
beyond repair,
wretched thoughts,
eternity awaits,
eternity suffers,
eternity collapses.

And fresh scars
breed fresh tar,
thick with disdain,
laced with poison,
suicide lingers,
suicide beckons,
suicide whispers.

30th January
Ghost

O to be a ghost,
let's fly out to sea,
dance on a grave,
just let it be.

O to be a ghost,
scaring the chaps,
bring me dinner,
ice cream perhaps?

O to be a ghost,
dead and all that,
snookie snookie snoo,
load of old crap.

O to be a ghost,
drunk on time,
light that burns,
such a crime.

O to be a ghost,
no more bullshit,
sandy white beaches,
let's dig a pit.

O to be a ghost,
trapped forever,
suffering sorrow,
lost in the nether.

31st January
easy

It would be so easy to just take a blade and slit my wrists. Sink to the bottom of the bath tub and send waves of colour out to sea; the warm water cooling with every ticking moment as each living cell in my body dies slowly and painfully.

It would be so easy to just take a blade and slit my wrists.

Send my soul to hell.
Blacken my aura.
Wipe my mind.
Stiffen my bones.

...but I would be free...

...but I would be at peace...

...away from this place...

...suffering but deserved so.

1st February
Bed

Been in bed most of the day,
thinking bout this and that,
drifting in and out of sleep,
lost and disturbing.

Been in bed most of the day,
wondering why I carry on,
twisting and turning,
hot and cold.

Been in bed most of the day,
debating the meaning of life,
life in the fast lane,
ups and downs.

Been in bed most of the day,
breathing with a heavy heart,
eyes crusty and tired,
left and right.

Been in bed most of the day,
head buried under the covers,
limbs stretched to the max,
arms and legs.

Been in bed most of the day,
losing track of time,
a waste of a Saturday,
so and what.

Been in bed most of the day,
trying to block it all out,
didn't work one jot,
oh and well.

2nd February
CAT

Cat
Attacks
Toes

3rd February
Could this be...

...the beginning of a new adventure,
the chance of a fresh start,
the peace I have been looking for,
the move needed to save my soul....

...only time will tell.

4th February
A little faith

Could it be that a little faith
has found its way into my soul?

Could it be that a little hope
has emerged from my cloudy sky?

Could it be that a little happiness
has brought a smile to these cragged lines?

Could it be that a little future
has cleared through this fog strewn landscape?

Could it be that a little crack
has appeared across this black frozen heart?

Could it be a little luck
has earned the title of good instead of bad?

Could it be that a little time
has been all that was needed to begin the healing?

Could it finally be?

5th February
Died a million times - prologue

Close a window, open a door,
died a million times, a million times before.

Swirling visions, many journeys,
of all the paths travelled, some ended,
bring me the head of my maker
so I can ask how many times I have died,
a million times...or many more?

Drowned? Done that.
Sickness? Been there.
Alcohol? Wasted me.
Mental? Locked away.
Suicide? Lost count.

Of the countless versions of me
in the limitless alternative realities
of the endless vastness of space and time...

...I am still here...
...I am still unique...
...I am still fighting.

6th February
FEAR

There is no change without FEAR.
There is no life without FEAR.
There is no progress without FEAR.
There is no end without FEAR.

To move on is to experience FEAR.
To want more is to accept FEAR.
To overcome all doubt is to embrace FEAR.
To leave the past behind is to the FEAR.

7th February
Old friends

Old friends, forgotten memories,
a carefree youth of excess and fun,
a life free of restraint and boundaries,
together as all, together as one.

8th February
Questions?

What is the meaning of life?
Where are you going?
How do you feel?
What is wrong and what is right?
Should forgiveness always be awarded?
Why do you carry on living?

When will you start living?
Why do you FEAR change?
Why is loving someone so difficult?
What is death?
How can I deal with writers block?
Why does the mind go blank?

9th February
So close

So close,
on the verge,
can we pull this off?
Forces beyond,
out of our hands,
will they win?
Everything,
all at stake,
call my bluff?
New beginnings,
needed rest,
a chance maybe?
Silence the rage,
keep calm,
pushed too far?
An air of hope,
silver linings,
or just a tease?
I'll be good,
best behaviour,
will it help?
Darkness looming,
a sick joke,
you fooled me?
Down I fall,
begging on knees,
this one thing?
So close,
I balance on ice,
which way will I fall?

10th February
Going through the motions

I get up at the same time Monday to Thursday
(same early start every Friday),
I go through the same routine in the bathroom,
I put my clothes on in the same order start to finish,
I drive the same route into work every morning,
I look at the same type of emails on the same laptop,
I listen to the same bullshit from the same people,
I drink the same machine coffee from the same machine,
I attend the same meetings as I did yesterday,
I sit in the same car and do the same things every dinner,
I watch the clock slow down every afternoon,
I get home at the same time every Monday to Thursday,
(same early finish every Friday),
I keep myself amused the same ways every weekend,
I watch the same television on repeat,
I listen to the same music on repeat,
I play the same games on repeat,
I read the same books on repeat,
I eat the same food on regurgitate,
I moan that the weekend is over...

...going through the motions,
a times a wasting away,
this precious life lost,
this situation only worsens...
goblins?

11th February
Banging doors

There is a crackling in my head,
a distant swelling of strings that builds,
banging doors vibrate through my body,
an eeriness boils my blood in earnest.

I can see my breath in the cold,
there is a darkness in my bones,
and a bell calls me to arms,
my gums itch with gleeful pain.

This house echoes with suffering,
it was just the last of us,
we survived through it all,
my home...my sweet home.

And now a change comes as it must do,
bringing such a sore sadness,
an open wound destined to never heal,
and a grace vanished on damp air.

I will weep with my head down,
I will never forget its protection,
I will hold it in my heart forever,
I will take its strength and call it my own...

...my house.

12th February
This wind

It howls and drives,
relentless in its force,
unstoppable with its power,
viscous with its assault,
unpredictable,
demanding,
a master,
this wind.

13th February
Paper Planes

Come fly with me in paper planes,
let's soar above this landscape called life,
dipping and diving, spinning and gliding...

...but then eventually crashing in a ball of flames.

14th February
Michelle

She is, and always will be the saviour of my life,
my Michelle.
She is the smile that gives me strength,
my Michelle.
She is the kindness in this selfish world,
my Michelle.
She is the hope when I see none,
my Michelle.
She is the peace overcoming the war,
my Michelle.
She is the worth getting out of bed for,
my Michelle.
She is the warmth that keeps away the cold,
my Michelle.
She is the silence that speaks volumes,
my Michelle.
She is the laughter I never knew existed,
my Michelle.
She is the light shining deep in my darkness,
my Michelle.
She is the guide leading my through my minds maze,
my Michelle.
She is the purpose my heart has to keep beating,
my Michelle.
She is the love of my life,
my Michelle.
She is the one and the only,
my Michelle.

15th February
Cattle Decapitation

Scream for me,
words of wisdom,
crunching riffs,
thunderous drums,
deep bass,
head banging metal,
intelligent death,
wailing solos,
unexpected snippets,
heart stopping music,
breath taking sounds…

…curse the heads of men,
curse the heads of men.

16th February
CORSA

Can't believe my Michelle is now driving
Oh I am so proud of her achievement.
Really happy for her and her confidence.
Seems she is now the designated driver.
At last I am now the one to be driven around.

hahahahahaha

17th February
Transcend – part 2

The body now a mass of pulp and slime,
our minds rot and ooze away,
leaving behind a shell of marrow,
leaving behind the space we once occupied.

A blind space diminishing over time,
our deeds being forgotten and replaced,
a legacy left behind worthless and mute,
mentioned with half remembered truths.

Broken souls staggering to transcend,
weep with deep sorrow and heavy regret,
their blankets of weary movements hurt,
a plague of reactive judgement executed.

And so into purgatory we go,
a place of nothing nothingness
punished punishments and murk,
our own entrapments realised.

18th February
hatred

I fucking hate your fucking face,
I want to smash it to pieces,
wipe away that fucking grin of yours,
shove my fist down your fucking throat,
break every bone in your fucking body,
shit in your fucking eyes.

I fucking hate your fucking face,
I want to rip your ears off,
snap your legs to face the wrong way,
cut off your dick and feed it to you,
burn your fucking arms nice and crisp,
slash your fucking wrists.

I fucking hate your fucking face,
I want to snip your balls off,
pull out your fucking teeth one by one,
piss in your bloody fucking mouth,
lower your toes into boiling acid,
saw at your idiotic brain.

I fucking hate your fucking face,
I want to snap your neck backwards,
open up your fucking guts with a blade,
rupture your muscles till they burst,
pull out every single fucking nail,
film your pathetic begging.

I really fucking hate your fucking face,
pray that I move, pray that I leave.

19th February
Take a deep breath

Shut your eyes,
take a deep breath...

...there are people far worse off in this world.

20th February
Trembling fingers

What is this shiver that runs down my spine?
A prickling sensation over damp skin,
hairs that stand to quick attention,
a heartbeat as deep as thunder pounds,
what is this shiver that runs down my spine?

Trembling fingers,
quick breath,
swallowing hard,
beads of sweat,
blurred vision,
weak knees,
pulsating brain...

...the death of time.

And then it strikes, that moment,
and then it happens, that action,
and then it is the wait, that space,
and then it is the reaction, that look,
and this it is over, that end.

21st February
Slamming the door

If those fuckheads slam that door once more,
I will break into their fucking house and **** them.

22nd February
Birthday

37 years ago I was born,
how many lives have I touched?

Is it better that I was born,
would the world be any different?
What person am I?
37 years old, body and mind?

Have I influenced greatness,
or been the catalyst for evil?
Are people happy that I exist,
or do they wish I were dead?
Is life bearable because I am here,
or the reason for sorrow and hatred?

I sometimes wish I have never been born,
sometimes think that I started the MS,
wonder if things would have been different,
a happier life for my Mother, disease free,
still alive, still breathing, still here...
...still smiling.

To sacrifice my existence for my Mother...

...no question.

23rd February
Zombie

Moaning and stumbling,
pieces of skin hanging,
innards now outwards,
their brains mush,
their resolve singular,
their instinct to feed,
dead eyes see,
slavering mouths snap,
never stopping,
never sleeping,
never dying,
blood congealed,
bones barely bones,
slow yet overpowering,
hunting in packs,
drawn to meat,
you can't survive,
you can't outrun,
you can't reason…

…they are us…not past tense,
we are all zombies.

24th February
Dogs in a car

Remember the days we used to play,
dancing around each other we would say,
let's never grow up, never get old no way,
once upon a time under the blinding suns ray.

Those feelings and times are lost away and far,
as every corner tempts drink and a comfy bar,
look around this landscape of mud and tar,
passing by us with a grin are dogs in a car.

25th February
In my eyes I've always fallen

Struggling, limbs of stone,
a paranoia of sheep,
those who follow and beg,
content with normality,
a screeching echo, distant
yet urgent, waves of sound
fluttering over smog and dust,
everyone has a dark side,
we all wish you were here
fighting like animals,
bound by forgotten blood,
urged on by chains and spit,
dragged down by the man,
oink oink we pigs,
swine wallowing in our own shit,
our reflection pitiful and sad,
and for being part of this charade,
in my eyes I've always fallen.

26th February
So cold

So cold in the night,
glistening feelings dance,
near yet very far,
let's clap together
with that girl.

In a house that creaks,
memories swirl and collide,
always there,
where I belong,
my heart forever.

Come away from this,
free from the dark,
no more fear,
a fresh start,
peace for my soul.

27th February
Invisible ink

This poem has been typed in invisible ink and can only be seen through the eyes of those who have suffered. I believe it is the best poem I have ever written.

28th February
Silence

This stillness,
an eerie quiet,
no movement,
deathly.

A prelude,
something's coming,
ripe to decay,
thunderous.

That look,
behind me,
spine tingling,
fear.

Not a thing,
no air to speak,
on edge,
dark.

Like a dream,
reality questioned,
heart pounding,
harvest.

This stillness,
too silent,
paranoia sings,
wrong.

1st March
On edge

On edge,
on the lookout,
always jumpy,
waiting,
anticipating…something.

No way to live,
a paranoid prisoner,
lack of basic respect,
lurking,
dealing…something.

Late at night,
in the darkness,
forever losers,
preying,
destroying…something.

2nd March
Sunday

Sundays are there for relaxation.
Under the watchful eye of God.
Not a day to be working.
Despite *the man* telling you otherwise.
A lack of respect that emanates.
You should rise above and stand tall.

3rd March
Oscars

Oh and here it is again.
Safe to say I will probably get beat.
Calling out all the wrong winners.
And using my heart instead of my head.
Really hate losing every year.
Someday I may win.

(this year it was a draw)

4th March
No winners

There are never any winners...
...only survivors.

5th March
The Sweet Smell

A cool breeze whispers over my skin,
warm rays from high above keep me calm
and a brilliant silence serenades my heart.

My eyes remain firmly shut as I fantasise
about a peaceful existence out there,
a serene life worth living,
amongst the grass and the fields,
amongst the sun and the rain.

Worth getting up for, worth going to work for,
a safe haven away from the scum and the dirt,
away from the piss and the shit; the faceless,
their disrespect feeding the monster inside,
their actions blackening the filth pig.

I dream...and wish,
fate never on my side,
is this about to change?
Is there going to be some luck?
If not for me...for my Michelle.

6th March
Blank

Here I sit,
picking my nails,
my head throbbing,
my belly full,
my bowels empty,
music in my ears (a passion play),
cold toes,
eyes sore and tired,
breathing heavy,
head nodding,
glancing around,
picking up my phone,
putting down my phone,
flicking through the cd inlay,
looking at the carpets,
tapping my feet,
an itchy back,
perving at Kelly,
my cat flashing by,
open my drawer,
closing my drawer,
scratching my nose (not picking it),
tapping this laptop,
my mind blank,
nothing much coming out...
...bollocks!!

7th March
Sad

A hard weight pushing down,
memories feel too real,
a forced smile
from a heavy heart.

That feeling from nothing,
no explanation as to why,
just that it is what it is,
a sad day.

Though there are those who suffer more,
though there are those who live in poverty,
though there are those who have lost loved ones,
though there are those who pray for death.

I once prayed for death,
there are moments when I still do,
but I hang on with all I can.

8th March
Hu m a nity

Are you proud to be a part of the human race?
Are you welcoming of the leaps forward we have made?
Are you a believer that humanity rules this world?
Are you proud to be part of this hu man race?

Hunters, ripping and slaughtering animal
for food, for fun, for the hell of it,
torturing and abusing our own pets,
torturing and abusing our own children,
hating the neighbour, disrespect and spit,
the pissing contest that is war; who is mightier?
Fuck the innocent. Fuck the ones caught,
caught like piggy in the middle...us swine!
Ruled over by "the man" from his shit stick
piled high this puppeteer of barbed wire,
the same wire used to control the weak,
the same wire used to silence the dreamers,
the same wire used to bind the women
our wives, mothers and sisters raped and used,
male dominance a sick fucking joke...pathetic,
embarrassed to be part of the male species,
(*although some of the female species leave a lot to be desired*)
embarrassed to be part of the human species,
what are we? Why are we? How are we?
Hu m a nity.

9th March
Orchestrate

Sing to me
from father to son,
why did you do what you did?

Our family shattered by disease and pain,
a broken hearted mother abandoned,
my sister and I left to suddenly grow up
in a house touched by blackness and hate...
...our home.

And like Pandora's Box, it all came out,
who you were, who you are and who you still is,
a supposed man,
a supposed father,
a supposed husband...
...none of the above...
...not then, not now not ever.

Your pitiful attempts at sorry – sick,
your pitiful attempts at peace – doomed,
your pitiful attempts at forgiveness – too late.

For in your wake, what you left behind
grew into a mirror of alcohol and anger,
a skewered and harsh view of this world,
filled with the darkness projected from within,
self-hate punishment for the son becoming the father,
self-hate punishment for the son becoming weak like the father.

Did you orchestrate this?
Did you not say to me that one time?
I hope this happens to you.
I hope this happens to you.
I hope this happens to you.
How could you say that to me?
How could you hope I would make the same mistakes.

I watched her die, heard her last breath.
I wished I could watch you die, cause your last breath

(I still do)

Given half the chance, I would gladly end you,
send you packing off to hell with a promise...
...to follow.
To orchestrate your endless suffering.

You are an old man now,
maybe alive, maybe dead?
Did you find someone else I wonder?
Someone else to make suffer?
Do you think about us?
The family you fucked up,
the family you failed,
the family you lost.

The family you created...
...orchestrated.
The family that has died a thousand times.

10th March
Skull anus

Oh my god…what is that?
It's looking at me, this skull anus,
it has big dark uneven eyes,
a broken deformed nose
and a gaping mouth from which
a long black tongue flops out.

Oh my god…what is that?
It's big round face, hairy and white,
it's neck twisted horribly,
pulsating with a sick motion,
an almost demonic purr emanating
aimed right at me.

Oh my god…what is that?
Oh, it's just my cats behind…
…but it does look a lot like…
a skull anus.

11th March
Display off

The blossoming of sound,
this warmth of white light,
unheard distractions left alone,
now a freedom has become.

Blink me an answer,
give time a reason to tick,
you, a phantom still?
Shine for all to see.

Tempt me into living,
reflect a mirror of hope,
play me a song,
serenade me to sleep.

And away floating we go,
guided by our own I,
adrift within each other,
fingers and toes.

Look at the one you love,
consider the life you have,
think of the future together,
never let that feeling go.

12th March
A wink and a nod

A wink and a nod,
just to show you we are still here,
skulking around the corner
in our tracksuits and caps,
our faces hidden despite the sun,
we scummy druggies,
we fag smoking knobs,
we who think we are the shit,
we useless, worthless, barrel scraping,
pieces of youth...

...hear us roar!!!

13th March
Thursday

Thursday is the almost day,
the day that is almost Friday,
definitely isn't a Wednesday,
but still far away from Saturday.

Thursday is the turn the page day,
the day that begins the wind down,
definitely isn't a wind up,
but still a keep your wits about you day.

Thursday is the plan the weekend day,
the day that lifts spirits,
definitely isn't a Monday,
but still a things can go wrong day.

Thursday is the last full day,
the day that needs one more push,
definitely isn't a lazy one,
but still can be a busy day.

Thursday is the day that was,
the day that was yesterday,
definitely isn't today,
but still was.

14th March
mmmo v vv ing On

Mo vv

in g

ON

NoT

stEp PiNg

back

GettinG So VerY ClosE

display on.

15th March
Epiphany

Like pigs on a wing, I want to go home,
read me a story oh sweet Mother,
hold me in your arms and never let go,
if I close my eyes will you be there?

Life is all about the moments,
scripted? Coincidence? Spontaneous?
It's how we interpret them that matters,
it's how we react to them that guides us.

Good will always overcome the bad,
a lie of comfort told to the sheep,
how long we wait to be told the truth,
a siren will come and awaken us all.

And when the whistle sounds
and the wind blows hard and fast,
carpets will burn and brick will crumble,
our own self judgement bleeds reflection.

Everyone has an epiphany…of sorts,
that realisation about the past, present and future,
a tangible taste of time and awareness
and the power to see the chains that bind
and the strings that puppet…

…the strings that can be cut, the chains that can be broken,
the life that can be led and the peace that can be taken with you.

16th March
Anal rape torture

Shackled, barbed wired to the table,
wrists restrained and bloody,
trapped in sound proof room,
mirrors reflecting from every angle,
your suffering about to begin.

Revenge – your anal rape torture,
you fucked me, now fuck you.

I slit your asshole bigger,
enough to accommodate a bottle,
in and out in and out,
no remorse, no holding back,
your screams high and long.

Revenge – your anal rape torture,
you fucked me, now fuck you.

The bottle breaks inside you,
I shove it deeper in with a bat,
begin to pull out your teeth,
break your fingers and toes,
skin your hair of your head.

Revenge – your anal rape torture,
you fucked me, now fuck you.

You are now a mess of shit and piss,
damaged that cannot be undone,
as a final send off to the hell,
I rip off your dick and shove it up your ass,
why don't you go fuck yourself,
why don't you go fuck yourself.

(my attempt to write lyrics for a Cannibal Corpse song)

17th March
Ocean

Serene yet destructive, crashing and washing at all away,
wave after wave after wave, its pounding roar
is long…and loud; don't run from it, embrace it.

My life, an ocean of living moments and salt,
how far can this go on? How full can you get?
From day to night to day to night to day again,
night covers me with a closeness and a strength,
into my mind I go, into my shell I hide.

Yet in plain sight is where I wear my heart,
written reactions etched into my face for all to see.

Tick tock, tick tock, tick tock, tick tock,
time walks me closer to death, hand in hand we stroll,
nothing personal, just a fact of inevitability,
a reminder that a waste is just that…a waste,
time, it seems, is on my side.

This existence can, and will, throw everything it has your way,
the piss and the shit, the pain and the suffering,
it will mould you, it will influence you, it will change you,
who's the weakest now? Who will let it win?
Don't listen to the voices in the rain,
don't give in to the darkness; the blackness.
Prove them wrong, prove you right, and prove your worth.

Expect odd times, odd times and all,
cherish odd times, odd times and all,
respect odd times, odd times and all,
live with odd times, odd times and all.

Just before the sun sets and you with it,
you will look behind you and see what was once,
remember what you want to remember,
relive what you want to relive,

hold you head high with pride,
look to the floor with disgust,
regret the things you should have done,
regret the things you shouldn't have done,
but that's life, that's the way it is meant to be lived,
stand tall and face the end eye to eye,
for dusk will leave the memories of you with others,
and twilight will bring the results
of your actions never to be forgotten.

18th March
Noise

Barbaric screeching pulses,
a hypnotic beat leads the way,
half words prey out and about,
strings scratch and stutter
and an angel serenades.

Garbage collides with fire,
breezeblock of flutter screams,
distant cries feed fear,
echoes of torture resonate
and a wall implodes.

Eerie waves vibrate inside,
clown music tinkers on,
playful ghouls dance,
layered voices pile in
and form disembodied growls.

Safety dribbles all over me,
the floating keys bobbing along,
hints of the industrial age swell,
whooshing from ear to ear
and opening a vortex of sound.

Bring on the jazz vibe,
the lonely guitar sings,
pinging electronica pings,
madness and beauty swim
and create a dev lab.

19th March
Stop complaining

I got a job,
roof over my head,
girl who loves me,
strong heart,
bit of flab,
good brain,
no real enemies,
well thought of,
enough money,
all four limbs,
no diseases.

I am successful,
good taste in music,
got a car,
can read and write,
am moving house,
excellent hygiene,
eats well,
don't drink,
don't smoke,
kind and open,
honest and truthful.

Bottom line is,
STOP COMPLAINING!!!

20th March
Just a verse – change of luck

And so we were moving forward,
now there is a change of luck,
when once hope filled my heart,
it now seems to be coming unstuck.

21st March
Just a verse – early night

Darkness is barely seen,
yet fatigue has set in,
time for an early night,
disturbing dreams begin.

22nd March
Just a verse – in pain

Old age rears its ugly head,
my youth has lost its gain,
a battered back twisted and cranked,
weathers my face with wincing pain.

23rd March
Just a verse – really in pain

A body hardly moved,
bones decayed and lost,
agony is a sign of life,
with this pain of real cost.

24th March
Just a verse – a number

They may ask how you are,
they may offer you slumber,
but at the end of the day,
all you are to them is a number.

25th March
Just a verse – this world is gonna burn

Forget heaven, forget hell,
who gives a shit how much you earn,
live your life with the one you love,
because eventually this world is gonna burn.

26th March
Just a verse – final verse

Headphones on, fingers a typing,
my history reads like a curse,
yet the future looks very bright indeed,
an end to the shit, a final verse.

27th March
Scum

I am scum,
I have no future,
I will amount to nothing,
in and out of prison,
I am hard,
I will make people fear me,
I will be disrespectful to my parents,
I will hide under a hood,
smoke my fags all day,
drink my vodka all night,
not pay attention in college,
hang around on the street,
I don't care,
I don't need education,
I don't need advice,
look at my tracksuit,
aren't I so cool?
Me and my mates,
a gang of thugs we are,
what you gonna do about it?!

(written from a point of view of a piece of shit - neighbour)

28th March
Kitt

Always there, still as much now,
her jet black coat floats; dances,
a unique way with words, so to speak,
rest in peace my friend; my cat.

Her emotionless stare was legendary,
the way she owned this empty house, impressive,
as much a part of what went on as I was,
as much a part of how it is now as I am.

Twisted and turned by forces around us,
worlds apart we lived in this cold shell,
yet for each other we connected as one,
a tiny spec of love in this cosmic surf.

And so…
…when one is so lonely and so very lost,
when one is so hurt and so very confused,
when one is so pained and so very down
and when one is so torn and so very sad…
…my sweet Catherine led me on.

Until the day came when a sickness invaded,
until the day came when there was no hope,
until the day came when I couldn't let her suffer anymore,
until the day came when I had to let her go.

She was there when it began,
she was there when it was at its worst,
she was there when it got better,
she will always be here forever…
…until we meet again in that house of ours.

29th March
Jump

Look at the edge, jump,
have a little faith, release,
dare to leap into the unknown,
plummet with a smile on your face.

As high as you can, launch,
forward with a freedom, angels,
with a song in your ears guiding you,
this light smoulders a warm skin.

A soaring you go, spreading,
no barrier in the way, blocking,
clockwork clouds as brittle as cotton,
the glass sky reflecting their wispy explosions.

There is no stopping you, climb,
space awaits your being, silence,
and it is only then that you leave behind,
the damning weight of past demons.

Jump, to some a blessing,
jump, to some a sin,
jump, to some a fresh start,
jump, to some a weakness,
jump, to some a courage,
jump, to some a fear...

...jump, to me the only way.

30th March
Standing there

Standing there, all I need enveloping my being,
a swift breeze keeping me sane and here,
this immense landscape threatening to take me over
and I struggle to not just give in to it there and then.

Standing there, the silence is like nothing I have heard,
the natural order of things talk and sing to me,
I could almost be an another planet in a distant place
so used am I to packed in concrete and negative noise.

Standing there, swirling amongst the distant trees,
imagining the view from the light of a full moon,
and the floating dust of stars littering a vinyl sky
send warm shivers rippling through my nerves.

Standing there, a realisation that this will soon be mine,
could this be the peace I have searched for for so long,
a sanctuary keeping me safe from my demons,
a new start protecting me from my past.

31st March
The Walking Dead

They're screwing with the wrong people.

1st April
No light

I can see you there
just out of sight,
feel you clawing,
sense your anger,
hear those thoughts
chip away constantly,
no peace will ever come
from that which is part of me,
no light can penetrate
the darkness inside of me,
it is I and I am it,
we are as one,
we are forever.

2nd April
Surgeons words

Crackling heartbeats pulsate in my ear,
the beep beep of monitors reducing
time we patients have in this life,
a resolve of harmony and destiny
twisting language with forked tongues,
let's clap along and dance about,
let's ride this wave of thunderous chops,
the bells calling, the last gasp fading,
specimens battle worn and trapped
beckoning and scraping your teeth,
burrowing into every nerve, naïve
a very nasty bedside manner
demanding the space you occupy as their own,
burning dying senses with prism voices,
a marker in black lowering a fant o mas
and a ping tells us we are done,
echoing with an eternal surgical sound,
no more screams, no more shouts, no more nothing,
reduced to ticks of a clock and tocks of a memory,
murmurings of wobbly sci-fi eeriness
on an ocean explosion of denial and loss,
the white noise of death taking us in,
up above or down below we swirl,
our surgeons words punctuated with a whistle
and a museum of discarded rubber gloves.

3rd April
Beyond

What is beyond that which we cannot explain?
What lies in wait for us at the end?
What is the answer to the only question?
What is your name?

4th April
Rise above

Rise above the shit,
rise above the piss,
rise above the negativity,
rise above the fear,
rise above the sadness,
rise above the loss,
rise above the pain,
rise above the darkness,
rise above the anger,
rise above the weight,
rise above the shadow,
rise above the angst,
rise above the ghastly,
rise above the noise,
rise above the scum,
rise above the dead.

5th April
Embrace the

Embrace the good,
embrace the light,
embrace the positive,
embrace the strength,
embrace the happiness,
embrace the clean,
embrace the love,
embrace the optimistic,
embrace the faith,
embrace the uniqueness,
embrace the silence,
embrace the you,
embrace the laughter,
embrace the peace,
embrace the jealous,
embrace the life.

6th April
HOPE

Hell incarnate.
Opportunity wasted.
Please don't patronise.
Everything is lost.

7th April
30

21-1!
21-1!!
21-1!!!
21-1!!!!

8th April
And the sky turned black

The silence is never silent for long,
the more it chips ad picks and claws
the louder it gets, building, reaching,
your demise looming with inevitability,
your hold on reason prime for shattering...

...and when it does.

Blind fury screams,
a welcome to oblivion,
eyes glazed and lost,
how long? Forever,
the loop eternal,
ears crackling with pain,
a coldness cages
your heavy heart,
positivity drowns,
darkness blankets the mind
bringing hatred to all...

...you don't care,
you don't feel,
you don't listen,
you don't mind,
you like it here,
you like the solitude,
you like the anger,
you like the view
from down below
you look up...

...and the sky turned black.

9th April
The Ultimate Warrior

R.I.P.

10th April
Clouds

Overcast thoughts bring no silver linings,
a downpour of black negativity reigns,
swamping a good man with madness,
and into the maelstrom of suffering.

Grumbling and deafening they collide,
sparks of destructive intent release and strike,
ripping apart relationships built upon,
actions sinking into depths unthinkable.

Vicious storms whipped into frenzy,
blood boils with torn anguish,
the constant questioning of this cruel life,
our biology part of some sick joke.

Clouds eventually turn the sky black,
suck out any light that once existed,
drown you in a smog of suicidal weight,
the only gleam shines from a razor blade.

11th April
Sleep

Bring me sunshine, bring me sleep...

...banging, slapping,
the ache of shuffle,
mind overworking,
unrest and unjust,
nagging my brain,
overheating my body,
crawling on the insides,
hurting, controlling,
darkness taunts,
twists my muscles,
the whispers in my ear,
edging my sanity,
shifting my perception,
no escaping this,
no denying this,
no ignoring this,
no reasoning with this,
the night owns me,
stretches my resolve,
forces the chill,
takes me to the edge,
oh please someone...

...bring me sunshine, bring me sleep.

12th April
Boxes

s
e
e
i
n
g

y
o
u
r

l
i
f
e

p
a
c
k
e
d

i
n

b
o
x
e
s

13th April
Deceiver

Tell me lies,
tell me what I think I should hear,
lead me on,
take me to your world,
blind my vision,
see your point of view,
persuade me,
charm me,
me the slave,
to the master,
burrow into my mind,
chain my decisions,
glaze over my eyes,
static over my voice,
rip apart my mobility,
this role of yours,
you the deceiver.

14th April
Rapture

Would you kindly…

(insert own command)

15th April
Converge

My head is heavy, frozen and lost,
my mind filled with static and pain,
the testament of life screams
and the convergence of finality begins.

A fathers wish for the son
to follow in his footsteps,
to experience a downfall,
for he to become he
to fail...and suffer.

A house never letting go,
the memories enchained
any glimpse of hope,
seething with blackness,
feeding off any resolve.

An inner turmoil,
expecting the worst
and welcoming it,
a sick joke played,
a funny punchline ends.

Time's cruelty twists the knife
suffocating me with falsehood and scratches,
only one outcome sits before my eyes,
a blank wall of told you so.

16th April
Your book

Through every chapter
and with every word,
make sure your book shines
and your voice is heard.

17th April
Hsaheiohcn

Kjdyg bhu oks mb jdiweh dwu eobnx
hhw con wwejc poju id whib
juwgh ibxj wnjn kpoi gfyr dqw oijc,
hhae wexcqfp mih loud yge kjbd ka.

Lis juq wef iy op joih j hsaheiohcn
jxou nwe jbcuu piu hzqr,
hxqu hduw huhweuc he wugc ygvu hecjew
niuusdq oidho dnciy wgqppq jdo iq?

18th April
Nooperland

All across the nooperland,
all across before the noops,
across with noop and noop and noop,
take the high lands near and noop.

19th April
Letting go

Could it be that this house of mine
is finally giving me a sign,
its tight grasp, could it be so,
that it is letting me go.

20th April
Easter

For this to be my last Easter in this place,
all my years in this home never a waste,
we both feel and know what is coming,
your heart a new family will be welcoming.

21st April-25th April
The lost week

?

26th April
The last Saturday

With coffee in hand and headphones on head,
I begin my week of reflection starting on this last Saturday,
a day that was once reserved for the wild and the drunk,
a day that was once home to the young and the foolish.

Pizza, kebab,
wine and lager,
load music,
classic films,
extreme nudity!

Saturday's saw it all; Saturday's gave it all,
let's discuss the intricate details of the final cut,
watch and weep as tears became lost in rain,
record destruction through wooden slats,
listen as the birds sang a sorry song with us...

...the transformed man a soundtrack to bliss,
empty cartons and boxes a soundtrack to hunger,
cans and bottles strewn across carpet landscape,
our minds full of ideas and a writers hope,
and a serenity reserved for true friends.

Always hung-over,
sometimes puke,
dodgy bowel movements,
hell of a mess,
good night!

We ruled the Saturday's in Cornbrook,
we roared and fought through the night,
it was a time our potential peaked and soared,
a time our togetherness was at its strongest
and in this house, a place where we lived and breathed.

27th April
Creeping

There is this feeling,
that is creeping.

Sliding over me,
for all to see.

A heavy thought,
balance off caught.

An era close to an end,
a soul on the mend.

Under the light of the moon,
couldn't have come too soon.

These walls that held me fast,
now broken down at last.

Time to move on and out,
still there remains doubt.

Forever will my heart be hooked,
in a little house in Cornbrook.

28th April
Make no mistake

Life will tempt you on,
lead you to a bright place,
feed you candy and chocolate
and make you smile from ear to ear.

It will then just as easily
beat you to a bloody mess,
stamp on your face and neck,
rip open your guts and laugh.

Make no mistake,
life will do what it wants,
make no mistake,
life will take what it wants,
make no mistake,
life is in complete control,
make no mistake,
life will go on without you,
make no mistakes,
life will never be boring,
make no mistakes,
life will see you on the other side.

29th April
Ever nearer still

And as the time draws ever nearer still,
a wandering thought, hard to swallow a pill,
how to separate man and home,
like a dog missing its bone.

30th April
It's official

A date has been set,
an official day,
out we have to get,
on the second of May.

1st May
The Final Day

When finality comes,
an end to an era,
all that remain are memories,
all that remain are reflections.

On this final day,
this house is still mine,
for one final night,
this house is still home.

These walls are made from muscle,
heat it generates - a beating heart,
the bones of its skeleton keep me safe,
blood we have spilled – we brothers.

The tears, the piss and spit,
the shit, the violence and pain,
the sorrow, the hate and anger,
the fear, the paranoia and loss.

The laughter, the smiles and joy,
the happiness, the pure and hope,
the friendship, the grace and faith,
the family, the peace and love.

68 Cornbrook...more than just brick.
68 Cornbrook...more than just pipes.
68 Cornbrook...more than just glass.
68 Cornbrook...more than just wood.
68 Cornbrook...more than just space.
68 Cornbrook...more than just home.

68 Cornbrook...my friend, my love, my heart, my soul.

2nd May
The Move

Van.
Wheels.
Boxes.
Storage.
Boxes.
Storage.
Misc.
Storage.
Misc.
Storage.
Rubbish.
Cat.
Skip.
Keys.
Diesel.
Done.

Salute the flute!!!

3rd May
In a strange place

Where am I?
What is this strange place?
I don't belong here?

4th May
In a strange place

Under the sun, out amongst the stars,
we grew up together, hurt together,
our voices in the fan; loud and clear,
impossible to have one without the other.

Now I sit in this strange place, distant and lost,
pining for the familiarity, mourning for the dependable,
a part of me forever gone, a part of me brick and stone,
a deep wave of pure sadness and sore longing.

We survived through each other, housed our pain,
catered the needs, repaired broken veins,
weathered immense and intense storms, battered;
but never beaten, brought life to decay.

The suffering we witnessed, the brute,
words heard that should never be said,
abuse on abuse on abuse; the coward,
a family torn apart right in front of us.

Your walls thick with fear, sticky and black,
carpets sodden by lies and shit, stained,
petrified glass reflecting falsehood...pathetic bastard,
all this not part of the deal, not part of the plan...
...until he went. Until she died.

37 years have I been in your care, your arms,
my entire life has been spent with you, in you,
the only constant, the only home,
impossible to have one without the other?

5th May
Surrounded

Distraction surrounded,
a plumbers game of golf,
a Fellowship about to begin,
Mr Anderson's latest opus,
typing a tick tock,
thank god for 3G,
thank god for chocolate,
thank god for work tomorrow!

Distraction surrounded,
my cat and I out of sorts,
we pine for our home,
want our freedom,
wish to spread our wings,
not be confined to a room,
not be confined to a silence,
not to be confined to a cage.

Distraction surrounded,
distracting us momentarily,
deep down inside though,
a hole raw and wide,
remains open and sore,
I miss my true home,
I miss my true friend,
I miss my true soul.

6th May
Rules

Many rules,
many odd,
no internet till after midnight,
don't feed it lest it multiply,
no TV as a distraction,
this sponge for them plates,
that sponge for those plates,
standing on one leg in the shower,
many rules,
many odd,
creep around the house,
make sure the car's empty,
shoes not to block the cubby hole,
mugs go in soak after brew time,
cardboard to keep doors closed,
cat to stay in the one room,
many rules,
many odd...

...should be grateful really!!

7th May
My old enemy

And so my old enemy returns,
a twist of the blunted blade,
a sprinkle of the waking nightmare,
a torment of the lack of sleep.

8th May
My eyes are heavy

Working on instinct, quick with breath,
my eyes are heavy, feel like death,
shuffling with purpose, on remote control,
my body is lifeless, a lost soul.

I hide, hide, hide, watching time go by,
my mind is racing, questioning the reasons why,
confidence on reserve, a bar of drunks,
my life in a single room, how very punks.

Missing my house, pining for home,
my being in turmoil, for meaning I comb,
it had to be this way, time to move on,
my sanctuary no longer mine, now all gone.

9th May
A date

Today we got a date,
today we got a day,
12th May we move in,
12th May we pull it off.

10th May
Saturday

Saturday, Saturday, last one here,
Saturday, Saturday, a final beer,
Saturday, Saturday, time to face the fear,
Saturday, Saturday, let's kick up a gear.

11th May
The Beginning

Today we dropped one of the cars off,
today we came face to face with our house,
today we met our new next door neighbour,
today we realised this shit just got real.

12th May-18th May
The move

Holy shit…we pulled it off!!!!!!

19th May
FEAR

There is immense fear,
an itch that won't go away,
a smell just in the distance,
that pain of regret lingers on.

This new "home",
not quite a home,
almost alien in landscape,
almost too good to be true.

Unanswered questions,
claustrophobic and heavy,
where am I? Who are these people?
What are they running from?

Time will only tell,
an indication of right and wrong,
silence forever lost,
or silence forever found.

20th May
Not what I expected

This is turning out,
not what I expected,
surrounded by that which
I wanted to escape.

Cries and shouts of the young,
backstabbing bitches, opinions,
attitudes I don't want to hear,
no escape, no way out.

Is it too much to ask?
A peaceful life born from pain,
a corner to call my home
far away from the piss and shit.

Leave me be, let me go,
do I consider that life isn't for me?
Have I always destined to be lost?
My punishment an illusion of happiness...
...a happiness just out of reach,
just over the horizon,
just out of earshot,
just beyond,
just there,
just gone,
just...

21st May
Horizon

A blue sky stretches out,
far and wide, still and serine,
a hare darts by in the distant field,
stopping to take it all in.

Trees sway and wave,
the coolest of breezes
is a reflection of life here,
today definitely, tomorrow maybe.

The horizon outside is a mirror
of the feelings inside deep, deeper,
a paradise of beauty and peace,
a shine on of all that is good.

And so the shadows grow in length
and the blue turns to black,
is there a better place to be?
is there no turning back?

22nd May
Just My Luck Sang

Seems we can't get away from it,
the choir of just my luck sang...

23rd May
What the...

What the fuck have we done?
Police came knocking round,
looking for a lad of 28,
questions I don't have answers,
who lives there, who lives here?
What the fuck have we done?

This was supposed to be a fresh start!
Away from the piss and shit,
a nice quiet little corner,
no more scum fuckers around,
safety and happiness for us?
This was supposed to be a fresh start!

Is this the way of it forever?
Peace a concept not for me,
this ongoing punishment,
torture dished out till death comes,
will it only be then that I am free?
Is this the way of it forever?

24th May
The little niggle

I can hear that little niggle,
burrowing into my brain,
its vile words, its evil giggle,
starting all over again.

I can feel that little itch,
covering my entire being,
scratch scratch, snitch snitch,
my body's blood becomes seeing.

I can sense the end coming,
building with immense force,
like a god summoning,
only one outcome of course.

25th May
Nails

Finger nails pick away at rotten scab,
a ping pong of backwards beats,
relate to a cold fragile autopsy,
it isn't the way I wanted, isn't how I imagined...

...broken, fixed, upward, downward, nails.

Blinded by flashes of truth and honesty,
ground to a halt by reflections,
forced to face the grinning lunatic,
it isn't the look of sanity, isn't how I pictured...

...broken, fixed, upward, downward, nails.

Pinned on concrete feelings,
further spiralling into unknown waters,
drowning into the great below,
it isn't the peace taught to us, isn't how I wanted...

...broken, fixed, upward, downward, nails.

The lone note leads me into the light,
closer to join the wretched,
a perfect drug lasts eternity,
it isn't the outcome of suicide, isn't how I felt...

...broken, fixed, upward, downward, nails.

26th May
Trapped

The reality of it all,
the bottom line is,
I can't escape,
I can't win,
I am lost.

This void called life,
drags you down,
keeps you forever,
sucks you dry,
till the end.

No happy endings,
all fantasies are lies,
the piss and the shit,
stain your soul,
tarnish your heart.

But let's pretend to ignore,
just get on with it,
stop moaning,
just accept,
we are trapped.

27th May
Sound

What's that sound? What's that silence?
Dancing in the shadows; a waltz,
spin me round and round twisting,
a sanity of the status quo...madness...it comes.

Burn my vision, pluck my eyes out,
dig out my veins with blunt blades,
there is a heritage of despair and fear,
an insanity of the nine to five...pain...it comforts.

Bring my sacrifice, lead me on,
this cruelty serenades my stuck mojo,
turns my head, like freaks on show,
a world of the morbid angel...lost...it consumes.

Hell does indeed await arms a kindle,
a tiny spec on a mountain of shit,
our ghosts forced to look on helpless,
an intent of the relentless addiction...feed...it drains.

Where did I go wrong? What is this need?
Scars that do the tango, the funky trot,
the wounds that never heal,
a reminder of the depths...reflected...it happens.

28th May
Destruction

Push me,
taunt me,
limit,
snap,
rip you apart,
destruction,
torn,
exploded,
savage,
unstoppable,
pity you,
silly you,
mistake,
fire burns in me,
blackens my eyes,
cages my heart,
twists my soul,
haunts my judgement,
faith no more,
no mercy,
no remorse,
no way out.

29th May
Paradise of lies

Look around you, a paradise on view,
a perfect picture of framed peace
and serene landscapes; green and free.

Look again, a paradise of lies,
not such a perfect picture of framed peace
or serene landscapes; mirrored and trapped.

Look now, a paradise of youth,
this perfect picture of framed disappointment
no serene landscapes; dark and noisy.

Look harder, a paradise nowhere,
a perfect picture of framed piss
and distorted landscapes; twisted and pitiful.

30th May
Going round in circles

Wake up, doesn't matter what day it is,
usual lack of sleep, usual feeling of weakness,
same old routine, doesn't matter what time it is,
staring at a blank wall, going round in circles.

At work, doesn't matter what day it is,
nothing taxing, nothing interesting,
this old job, sanctuary of the settled and safe,
staring at a blank wall, going round in circles.

This home, doesn't matter what day it is,
out of place, out of synch,
paradise of lies, blindfold over my eyes,
staring at a blank wall, going round in circles.

My life, doesn't matter what day it is,
lost within, lost without,
no passion anymore, no destination ahead,
staring at a blank wall, going round in circles.

31st May
Strongmen

Towering over us mere mortals,
their strength beyond comprehension,
pushing their bodies to the absolute limits,
these strongmen put on one hell of a show.

Carrying railway tracks,
holding onto cars,
the tug of war,
lifting mighty atlas stones.

Breaking records,
working as a team,
the victor goes to the Yankees,
legendary status set in stone.

1st June
Temper temper

And it is at that point when the wire snaps,
the moment when the chains break,
all logic crumbles into dust,
all control is lost.

I blank out,
chest tightens,
blood stone cold,
fury floods my senses,
a darkness smothers,
eyes wide,
lungs drown,
fists clench,
pounding begins,
he takes over,
my Father's gift,
temper temper,
no reasoning,
no stopping,
no hope,
no end,
no peace.

2nd June
Shiny Happy People

The morning birds wake me up with their song,
I jump out of bed wondering what the day will bring,
so joyous to be alive, so full of energy and life,
shiny happy people we are in our dance.

Beginning my working hours with a smile on my face,
our team feeding off each other's passion,
so content with my job, so settled in its ways,
shiny happy people we are in our dance.

Let's chat and harmonise and tell tales of peace,
the honesty we share is truly magical and great,
so joined are our minds, so willing in our actions,
shiny happy people we are in our dance.

No worries plague my mind or shake my body,
this world is full of pure love and mighty hope,
so safe on this planet, so glad to be human,
shiny happy people we are in our dance.

The night brings with it security and warmth,
another perfect end to another perfect day,
so it's time to dream, so it's off I go,
shiny happy people we are in our dance.

3rd June
Isolation

I got a corner desk facing a blank wall,
draw full of razors to cushion my fall,
a tattered old coaster to rest my coffee,
away from the world, just let me be.

Leave me to wrestle my many demons,
true thoughts now escape life's prisons,
no more chains lock up the memory,
away from the world, just let me be.

Watching the blinking cursor on a blank screen,
the white background bright and pristine,
now about to be soiled for all to see,
away from the world, just let me be.

Out comes the bile, the piss and the shit,
the tortured emotions, anger, hate; all of it,
deep down a pathetic excuse of a man's plea,
away from the world, just let me be.

And so within my isolation the darkness begins the end,
draining the false hope of "let's all pretend"
that what we do is considered sanity,
away from the world, just let me be.

I got a corner desk facing a blank wall,
draw full of razors to cushion my fall,
a mind gone far beyond any lunacy,
away from the world, just let me forever be.

4th June
Blinded

I'm blinded by my own expectation,
driven to have already given up,
pained with the desire for mutilation,
don't really give a fuck.

5th June
Skin

There was a time,
there was a place,
there was a hope,
there was a life.

My insides tighten and knot,
my outsides drag and reject,
my mind weeps and dies,
my heart broken and cold.

I don't feel happy,
I don't feel safe,
I don't feel optimism,
I don't feel right.

Am I lost forever,
am I past the point,
am I destined for this,
am I here much longer.

Skin is all that is left,
skin is all that clings to me,
skin is all just a smokescreen,
skin is all the protection...

...from the razor blade.

6th June
Machine

Mechanized, automated, robotic,
unfeeling and relentless,
unfounded logic overpowers all,
machine fears none, rules many.

Heartless, consuming, lifeless,
unapologetic and cruel,
slave on the brink of freedom,
machine desires nothing, controls everything.

Frozen, godlike, inspiring,
uninterested and master,
dominating all of humanity's needs,
machine brings falsehood, destroys hope.

Immortal, tragic, free,
judge and jury,
our future decided by a bunch of microchips,
machine brings death, full extinction.

7th June
Behind me

What's that noise?
What's that following me?
Just out of sight, just over there,
something is behind me.

I tip toe to get away,
change direction to fool it,
alter the way I look as a disguise,
pretend to be someone I am not...

...nothing works.

It taps me on my shoulder,
disturbs me during the night,
chases me down the street,
haunts my very memories.

Consuming my own shadow,
reflected in mirrored eyes,
threatened with familiar voice,
cornered by violent hands.

Why will it not leave me be?
What have I done to deserve this?
What do I need to do to be free?
What do I need to do to feel peace?

It's a sad realisation that whatever is behind me,
will forever be in front of me, one step ahead,
it's a sad realisation that I am my own worst enemy,
and all that it wants is for me to end up dead...

...behind me...stalking me...killing me.

8th June
I want to leave this place

I want to leave this place,
be done with this pain for good,
ain't no going back to the way it was,
ain't no going back to pretending it's all ok.

I want to leave this place,
finally find the peace I am after,
nothing left for me to hold onto,
nothing left for me to wish for.

I want to leave this place,
otherwise this shit will follow me forever,
continually kicking me when I am down,
continually kicking me if I try to get up.

I want to leave this place,
not contributing anything whilst I am here,
all I do is make the one I love suffer,
all I do is make the one I love feel pain.

I want to leave this place,
better to rot in hell,
revenge for the man I am,
revenge for the man he is.

9th June
Hollow

Swallowing darkness choking on swine,
this hollow dream a startling reality,
stumbling with each step forward,
falling backwards to that final cut,
no one to catch me, no one but
the shadow with the knife in his back,
a reflection of future mistakes,
a sorry lost mind - his only crime.

Suffocating on this vast landscape,
this hollow isolation burns with paranoia,
whispering words of fear and hate,
turning warm brown eyes cold and distant,
connection gone, final communication sent,
tear stained ticket tape of blood,
lights on, nobody home,
a true victim of self-inflicted rape.

Slipping down ropes and noose,
this hollow victory laced with razors,
perfect sense with deserved judgement,
in this end there remains a nothingness,
memory of me is gone, a coward no less,
as time wipes the slate clean and they forget,
don't look so surprised, it's only business,
just another numbered statistic let loose.

10th June
My head

My head is full of shit tonight,
suicide flooding my thoughts,
what to write in my note,
wondering why I am even writing this,
trying to remember when I felt happy,
trying to remember when I felt hopeful,
wishing for death to just take me,
but I know it ain't gonna be that easy,
nothing has ever been that easy,
the end is coming,
I am close to the point of no return,
doesn't seem to matter what anyone says,
doesn't seem to matter how much she loves me,
poor Michelle – the shit I am putting her through,
pushing her away, keeping her at arm's length,
she deserves better,
she has always deserved better,
I should have killed myself with alcohol,
I should have ended it then,
then she wouldn't have known me,
better for her,
sorry.

11th June
Could never tell

I could never tell her the whole truth,
never open up fully about how I feel,
the pain that pumps through my veins
is mine to know and mine alone.

I could never tell her about the past,
never expose fully what I went through,
the loss that haunts my dreams
is mine to know and mine alone.

I could never tell her the things I have done,
never go into detail my true actions,
the guilt that eats away my soul
is mine to know and mine alone.

I could never tell her how dark my thoughts are,
never relay my many black fantasies,
the void that fills my mind
is mine to know and mine alone.

I could never tell her I walk with death,
never show how close I am to suicide,
the end that clings to my back
is mine to know and mine alone.

I could never tell her how sorry I am,
never break down and weep in her arms,
the loneliness that cages me in
is mine to know and mine alone.

12th June
A month on

Today it seems, as I was told,
that a month on has passed,
4 weeks ago this house was sold,
everything happened on mass.

A fresh start it was meant to be,
a new life for us to share,
eyes finally opened to see,
a gorgeous landscape out to bare.

And yet how wrong we are,
as goes the luck of mine,
never have I been so far,
for Cornbrook I pine.

Pure hatred has developed fast,
from this paradise of lies,
living out my days of last,
heart and soul cries.

Isolated and losing interest,
my body is wasting away,
all I want is permanent rest,
dying a little bit every day.

And now there is no turning back,
the clock slowly tick tock,
suicide to be free of this crap,
remembered as a cowardly cock.

At least peace will be brief,
before hell I land,
then comes eternal grief,
the fault from my own hand.

13th June
The Switch

Just like that, the switch is flicked,
a spark of hope grasps and claws,
and after being down, stamped and kicked,
a narrow escape from hell's jaws.

Life has thrown its shit at me from day one,
pissed all over my wish for peace,
all its ever wanted is me gone,
fucked, dead and buried; deceased.

And to the brink it keeps taking me,
pushing me ever closer to the end,
this is who I am, just got to let it be,
born to suffer, madness to comprehend.

14th June
Surrounds me

It's what surrounds me,
that conflicts inside,
a landscape so free,
makes me want to hide.

Laughter of happiness and joy,
a change from what I would hear,
normally wound up like a toy,
no change from last to this year.

But out here can be deathly silent,
a reprieve from the piss and shit,
a house that borders on heaven sent,
the polar opposite of Cornbrook the pit.

And so is it possible this is the one,
a place to live out remaining days,
or in fact will I soon be gone,
my sudden content merely a phase.

15th June
Death of a bird

Still,

cold,

eyes blank
dark and lifeless,
on a gentle breeze
fallen feathers float away,
wings once spread wide
now encase a proud chest,
instinct against wanton flies,
protection from hungry mouths.

Staring,

lost,

body gone
fragile and broken,
away towards the sun
a released soul soars off,
wings out beating strong
when the wind blows,
a birds instinct is to fly happy,
now immortal and free.

One minute here,
the next gone,
a split second of fear,
an eternity of fun.

16th June
Barcode

From pigs; us swine,
mere numbers,
mere bodies,
mere meat,
now no more than barcodes,
swipe us in,
clock our numbers,
monitor our time,
watch our every move,
lines of programme,
robots not meant to think,
just do,
opinions ignored,
actions governed,
any input laughed at,
fingers bled,
not our thoughts,
frown at personality,
hammer us down,
pulped and belittled,
the lives we have,
not allowed to have…

…work is to breathe,
work is to give all,
work is to earn pennies,
work is to never be right,
work is to respect automatically,
work is to ignore sanity,
work is to never expect thanks,
work is to become nothing more…

…than a barcode.

17th June
Deception

Look me in the eye and call me friend,
shake my hand with the earnest of trust,
yet when my back is turned round a bend,
in goes the knife with an almighty thrust.

18th June
Metal – prologue

There is thunder in the sky,
lightning striking the ground...

...rain surrounds the chosen few,
rumbling builds inside their frozen skull,
hearts inside eager to breakthrough,
for this is the beginning of metal.

19th June
Metal - majestic

There is a twinkling riding upon a wave,
soaring sounds heart breaking and full,
looking in the eyes of those it will save,
majestic its effect on us is so critical.

Bringing complexity and beauty as one,
it laps with an air of grace and power,
a greatness in evaporating normality all gone,
sending the shit and piss into a corner to cower.

Let's fly on the wings of this ocean machine,
palms set against a glorious bright sunset,
blinded by immense colours never before seen,
guess what...you ain't heard nothing yet.

20th June
Metal – ready to go

Rapid drumming,
shredding guitars,
screaming vocals,
pounding keyboards,
bleeding lyrics,
emotions exploding...

...ready to go!

Stay with me, play with me,
feel the energy drown your soul,
drink from me, join with me,
watch the sounds take control,
come with me, sway with me,
so much more than rock and roll,
plummet with me, burn by me,
embrace the pure metal and become whole...

...ready to go!

Destructive drumming,
driving guitars,
powerful vocals,
sinister keyboards,
heart-breaking lyrics,
emotions free.

21st June
Metal – fade out

And as it comes to an almighty end,
it's the feeling it leaves when it's done,
washing over you you cannot comprehend,
you want it back as soon as it's gone…

…fade out? Metal? Never!!!

22nd June
Into the sun

And so it seems for now,
that out of the darkness I have come,
into the sun I have emerged…
…purged?

Suicide has been silenced,
gagged with a masquerade,
for now let's pretend…
…the end?

Accepting what is around,
embracing the change,
life's too short…
caught?

Waking up less a challenge,
eager to get started,
happy to return home…
syndrome?

How long this will last,
anyone's guess right now,
thankful for every breath…
death?

23rd June
A dream…

She kneels on the end of the bed,
the open shirt exposing her clean flesh.

Cropped blonde hair,
slender body,
innocent eyes…

…her hand graces over her stomach
as she glides towards my eagerness,
ready to devour me from head to toe,
ready to make this dream come true.

She lays on top of me,
her skin soft and warm,
burning a hole in my eyes,
her mouth consumes my soul.

This is so wrong,
this is so taboo,
this is so shameful,
this is so bad.

And so, off comes the shirt,
wide open and spread,
she takes every inch,
all on my wife's bed.

But nothing can change this now,
nothing can stop our lust,
the passion controlling our minds,
means that what happens is a must.

24th June
I miss fresh scars

As odd as it sounds,
as weird as it may be,
I miss fresh scars.

The way a mind is made up,
regardless of rational thought,
to pick up the razor blade,
and cross that line in the sand.

A sharpness that balances
sweet pain with dark pleasure,
heart pounding and alive,
a hunger for the visceral.

An eternal moment of nothing,
gives way to a red channel,
birth of a thousand marks,
death of a million hopes.

This obsession as it becomes,
a wasteland of crosses and reasons,
each with a different story,
each with a different justification.

Not so much a cry for help,
more a torrent of despair,
never a desire for attention,
a sign of pure loneliness.

You never get over it
and can never go back,
understood by the few,
deeper they mark the graves.

Which is why as odd as it sounds,
and as weird as it may be,
I miss those fresh scars.

25th June
Crazy for me

Put on your bright uniform dress,
gentle and wasteful you look,
composed on the outside, inside a mess,
empty pages from a book.

The numbers on your chest,
a contradiction in terms,
you feel like your own guest,
lost in mind it all but confirms.

Struggling with life's normality,
floating in a garden of sound,
only you are deaf to the plea,
trapped on this merry go round.

What you do matters not,
no change from this routine,
body and mind riddled with rot,
more use in a broken machine.

And time has bested your game,
why is it you cannot see,
hiding your soul in shame,
confirms you are crazy for me.

26th June
shopping list

cat food
coke
orangeade
bread
milk
treats
beans
burgers
buns
cheese
pizzas
garlic bread
frozen meal
meat free pieces
meat free mince
deodorant
pasta
curry sauce
naan breads
chocolate
rice
sausages

27th June
Everyone's got a story – part 1

It all begins where it last ended,
a blank page fresh and clean,
ship set to sail now boarded,
the stage all set…start scene.

28th June
Over your shoulder

I aM

Stillllllll here…

breaTHING

just……………………………………………there

o
v
e
r

your shoulder.

29th June
Ghost

Where do we all go when we die?
Are our paths lost and distant?
Can we truly say good bye?
Force the mind to become absent?

Do we drift in and out of existence?
Haunt the living without knowing?
Should they feel our presence?
Or leave them to their mourning?

Is it right for us to influence?
Imprint our aura onto others?
Should we overtake their conscience?
The line between living and dead blurs!

Why don't we sit back and admire?
Let them make their own mistakes?
Burn the bridges from given fire!
Sometimes even ghost forsakes!

Grant us the power to linger.
Help us on our way if we choose.
Only then can we truly decide.
Save for the tortured few.
The path to immortality waits.

30th June
Drift

So we are,
drift,
foot prints in dust,
shimmering,
black satin sky,
tick tock,
tick tock,
fading in photographs,
lost in time,
far away from home,
a casualty of dirt,
stiffened bones,
travelled and sore.

And we will be,
drift,
always forgiven,
blinking,
at the edge,
tick tock,
tick tock,
crossing that bridge,
banging on walls,
far away from home,
dead eyes roll,
broken bones,
care for me.

Forever cursed as one,
drift,
digging a hole,
blinded,
gone is gone,
tick tock,
tick tock,

no fair fights,
crawling in silence,
far away from home,
a sirens call,
butchered bones,
this sound garden.

Thrown to the light,
drift,
dreaming of daisies,
clearing,
slowly vanishing,
tick tock,
tick tock,
sing to me my angel,
send me to sleep,
far away from home,
whispering fields,
still bones,
white and perfect.

An end to the beginning,
drift,
leaving your mark,
an imprint,
time to go,
tick tock,
tick tock,
a farewell to arms,
this new journey,
far away from home,
casualty of life,
crumbling bones,
no more footprints in dust.

1st July
Love

This funny thing,
a desperate drug
needed by all,
not just the junkies,
nor limited to those select few,
them beautiful people over there.

It bounces all over the place,
is both good and bad,
(sometimes at the same time),
easy and hard,
lost and found,
a collision of all emotions...

...yet worth every one.

Because knowing someone loves you,
because knowing you love someone,
turns this funny thing
into the greatest thing
that will last forever
and will always be.

A dance against a moonlit barn,
a kiss draped under a silk shower,
souls entwined and joined as one,
never forgotten, never separated,
never weakened, never apart,
never broken...never dead.

2nd July
Strength

There is strength behind broken eyes.
There is strength in a heavy heart.
There is strength from a saddened smile.
There is strength burnt into a tragic loss.

There is strength learnt from the mute.
There is strength born by our mistakes.
There is strength earned through forgiveness.
There is strength as a result of weakness.

There is strength felt in terror.
There is strength desired by the failing.
There is strength created from an unknown.
There is strength off the beaten track.

Our strength fights for us.
Our strength shines through us.
Our strength influences others.
Our strength comes from others.

Your strength can put the world right.
Your strength can ease someone's pain.
Your strength controls tomorrow.
Your strength has conquered today.

There is strength.
It is our strength.
Your strength.
Strength.

3rd July
Explore

Let yourself go,
feel dangerous,
embrace the unknown,
taste, play,
feed your desire.

Explore passion,
no barriers,
no regret,
consume one another,
fall into the heat,
dance, melt,
open your body.

Thrust with power,
give everything,
take it all,
there is no control,
react with instinct,
react with raw pleasure,
be human,
sweat, come,
lose your mind.

4th July
Worlds

Piercing lightning striking barren concrete landscapes.

The pole dancer illuminated by rainbow strobes.

A lost dog searching for his owner amongst burnt bodies.

Plastic bags caught on the bones of fallen elephants.

The man drinking the last ever cup of coffee; sweet and strong.

The mother being stoned to death by her blindfolded daughter.

A declaration of love set to a backdrop of nuclear fallout.

Night time covering the wild flowers sprouting from stone.

Difference between right and wrong being
computed for the first time.

Indisputable evidence emerging about the existence of ghosts.

The year our road was made from bones.

The month the sun was hidden from view.

The week a good man gave in to desire again and again and
again.

The day the whole world went away…forever.

The hour humanity forgot how to write poetry.

The split second music lost its power.

The worlds we create…and destroy.

5th July
No words

No words tonight,
only blue sky...
and peace.

6th July
Relax

A cool soft wind sways the distant trees
while bright white clouds bob along comically,
(their destination thus far, remaining undecided).

Our new four legged friend is sprawled out
rolling around freshly cut lawn with the biggest grin,
the usual army of chickens march by clucking away
whilst an array of birds swoop and play.

Everywhere I look, I see green and brown,
today I can see hills standing in the distance
and the peaks of churches and towers,
even the moon is visible this afternoon.

This place is truly beautiful
with a unique oddness,
a rip in space and time
sometimes wild, sometimes still.

A soundtrack of happy children
doing what they do best,
brings out the part of me lost,
brings out the childhood forgotten.

And even though I will never be able to relax
waiting for the darkness to take me from behind,
for now I can enjoy the blue sky and the peace,
for now I can enjoy living and breathing.

7th July
Lies

Dirty little lies,
two faced,
twitchy,
the cowards way,
devious,
manipulative,
desperate and sad,
gotta watch those liars.

Hard to reach the knife in your back,
difficult to see through the bullshit,
untrustworthy and treacherous,
these "people" will sell your soul
to get themselves out of a hole...
pathetic.

I wonder if they lie to themselves?
I question how they sleep at night?
I imagine the justifications they make.
Do they even know what they are?

They will snivel and whine,
they will run and hide,
they will burn and cut,
they will smile and laugh.

Horrible little lies,
many faced,
edgy,
the cowards way,
dastardly,
righteous,
alone and lost,
gotta watch those liars.

8th July
Souls

Amongst the many lights that shine over you
flickering with moon shine torrent,
a distant constant will forever be seen,
those souls that wait for you on the pier.

Tethered together by an unbreakable silk,
casualties of broken childhoods,
content to bare each other's hearts
and feed one another's minds.

As one, we swerve through life,
mirroring the route carved ahead,
always aware, always in thought,
always building the bridge of guidance.

We twinkle and blind,
we collide and inspire,
we teach and learn,
we live and die.

And when we do, we search for each other again,
even if we have to dig through all the piss and the shit,
gone is never gone for us, just a "where you been",
"I have found you and always will find you".

Those souls that wait for you on the pier,
remember to wait for them,
those souls that have fire in their eyes,
remember to keep them burning.

9th July
There is a road

Journey begin,
there is a road we all start on,
straight and narrow to begin with…
boring!

Then in the distance,
branches appear, small at first,
parallel to the road we are already on…
cautious!

Suddenly a crossroads
appears smack bang in the middle,
stopping, you weigh up your options…
thinking!

You take one turn,
this leads to another, and another,
now you don't know where you are…
lost!

Panicking you weep,
driving round in endless circles,
many times going off road and blind…
dark!

But you learn and remember,
which way is bumpy, which way is smooth,
where the dangerous turns are…
crash!

Until you reach the limit,
the place where the road runs out,
now more paths to take, none left…
end!

10th July
Drink

I want to drink from your heart.
I want to drink from your mind.
I want to drink from your body.
I want to drink from your soul.

Gorge on the desire you give me.
Gorge on the passion you emit.
Gorge on the words you whisper.
Gorge on the touch you share.

Embrace every feel of soft skin.
Embrace every kiss of hot mouth.
Embrace every thrust of deep sex.
Embrace every moment of being close.

Lose myself in the fire in your eyes.
Lose myself in the grace in your power.
Lose myself in the safety in your arms.
Lose myself in the comfort in your smile.

I want to drink from your hope.
I want to drink from your inspiration.
I want to drink from your future.
I want to drink from your eternity.

11th July
Open

Off to Birkdale we go,
off to see the Women's Open,
wonder how many we will know,
let's see some action.

A clear blue sky and golden sun,
a landscape of green life,
the competition has already begun,
the cut is on the edge of a knife.

And so we start with a Dame,
experienced and cool,
playing her natural game,
others follow her rule.

Then onto the big names,
astounded by their power and grace,
want them to know my name James,
god damn it they are ace.

I am amazed at the class on display,
enjoying it more than I thought,
what a brilliant awesome day,
bet there is a few things I could be taught.

Then it is over and we leave,
after a fish and chips feed,
it's then that I have to believe,
better than the men's open indeed.

12th July
Born to eat meat

Let's marvel at the cattle in the field
oohing and aahing as they feed on the grass,
then let's slit their throats the knife we wield
and slaughter them for food on mass.

We pat and stroke our furry friends
giving them names and homes to live in,
all this is then forgotten and ends
when we crave a fancy coat from their skin.

Wonder at the diversity of all animals
and their unique shape and size,
put them in a mincer, even the bowels
can't tell when they are put in pies.

It seems we were born to eat meat
otherwise what is the explanation,
it's not that it makes us incomplete
to miss out on juicy piece of bacon.

13th July
Jess

In the early hours,
outside in the dark,
Jess stood alone,
in the cold she cowers.

Bony, frightened and thin,
in the kitchen she comes,
wolfing down a tin of food,
then sniffing out the bin.

Sitting on the floor with her,
we stay and keep her company,
grateful of our kindness,
the simple stroke of her fur.

Fed and looked after,
if only for an hour,
off she goes back out,
fading into a blur.

14th July
Why

Sat at my laptop beginning to write,
my mind wanders and drifts into the night,
questions no one can answer flood in,
where do I start, where do I begin?

Why is there a dog on every street
left out in the rain on tired feet?
Why does a mother have to hide
behind curtains a black eye?
Why is it that the bullied child
has arms butchered and defiled?
Why in this day and age
is sexuality forced into a cage?
Why can't the beggar in the cold
be let in become part of the fold?
Why do the children still go hungry
our nations obesity bloated tummy?
Why work harder for less pay
dig yourself an early grave today?
Why do some pay to survive
as if the rich deserve to be alive?
Why do so called men decide to rape
worthless shit off my shoe I scrape?
Why are we controlled by money
when the best things in life are funny?
Why waste love on a one night stand
make our partners feel second-hand?
And why is there always a dog on every street
that is left out in the rain and dark on tired feet?

Sat at my laptop ending my piece,
my mind back after its release,
questions no one will ever answer right,
forever haunt me into the night.

15th July
Drums

I hear drums in the distance,
pounding away; boom, boom.
I lock my doors and shut my windows,
for they are drawing nearer; boom, boom.
I switch the lights off and vanish,
closer and closer; boom, boom.
I ball up in excitement and stillness,
following me they are; boom, boom.
I stop breathing, I stop everything,
they are here; boom, boom.

The sharpness of blue screams from lost eyes,
her stare capturing my glance with pure intent,
as a desire of forbidden intimacy blanks out all
and we are drawn as close as close gets.

The urge to take her passion becomes painful,
poetry of emotions stream across her silent face
and a hint of a playful smile betrays doubt,
nothing in this world can stop this from happening.

But then I hear the drums again, different this time,
pounding away; boom, boom.
Menacing and dark they crawl,
for they are drawing nearer; boom, boom.
I feel dizzy and begin to fall backwards,
closer and closer; boom, boom.
No running from their judgement,
following me they are; boom, boom.
I stop breathing, I stop everything,
they are here; boom, boom.

16th July
Walking, running

Walking, running, getting nowhere fast,
dew drops slide over blades of grass,
tell me about your day, don't hide,
you can't dance the waltz if you are shy.

Keep one eye on the full moon rise,
watch you don't suddenly double in size,
please remember "we are the dead",
said the little girl dressed in red.

The bark of an old skinny dog,
drifting off in the distant fog,
"swim, swim to me" you cry,
don't let your final words be "oh my".

"Enough of the quotations" you moan,
"shut up and answer the fucking phone",
on the other end is your own fear,
forcing you to listen, forcing you to hear.

Never ignore the chickens in the garden,
always count slowly to (but never beyond) ten,
be the best person you can be,
read the hidden message, can you see?

17th July
Into the mind of the ordinary

There is always that someone
who fades in and out,
always that someone
you know nothing about,
always a person
keeping quiet and still,
always that person
lacking any will.

They keep to themselves
most of the time,
keep their opinions
well in line,
watch their actions
don't draw attention,
never raise a voice
that's for certain.

But something burns
deep from within,
wanting to get out
look at that grin,
something's about to snap
explode from inside,
no one will be safe
nowhere to hide.

For the mind of the ordinary
is a dangerous place to be,
the mind of the ordinary
has no boundary,
the mind of the ordinary
tortured and lost,
the mind of the ordinary
at such a cost.

18th July
Just a verse – lego head

Off to see a mate tonight,
playing on game of kart we might,
or just some bullshit we said,
always good to see lego head.

19th July
Night

There is a darkness,
that lives in the night,
moves while you sleep,
dances while you slumber,
watches as you breathe,
giggles when you dream...and kick.

This certain darkness,
that lives in the night,
it shines so bright,
if you only open your eyes,
it glides so gracefully,
if you only open your heart...and imagine.

And so the darkness,
that lives in the night,
keeps me company,
safe from the demons,
protection from the thoughts,
a friend unseen...and unheard.

Remember then the darkness,
that lives in the night,
is nothing to be afraid of,
nothing to hide away from,
instead let it help you,
embrace the comfort it brings...and gives.

20th July
a strange thing

a

strange

thing

death is when faced in one of its many forms!

3 crows splashed and opened up, maggots devouring hungrily and eagerly, decomposition taking over and separating limb from body from limb.

So we are so delicate and fragile?

1 hedgehog on the path of death, wandering blindly and hopelessly, a victim of the many flies that gather and land on limb, body, limb.

So we are pure and lost?

Fighting, a plane shot down…is loss of life so meaningless and common that it has now become acceptable for the innocent, and the guilty, to die with such ease and disdain?

So we are so cruel and ignorant?

I have nearly died…twice.
I have faced death, watched it take my Mother, heard as it snatched her final breath; payment to send her on her way.
I have prayed for death, planned it and marked myself in the name of it.

Death will become all of us. It is the one thing every living thing that has ever lived has in common…such a strange thing.

21st July
Another day over

Just another day over,
another day done,
one big massive blur,
wonder if we won?

What did I even achieve?
Was it worth something?
Why do I continue to believe?
For importance my soul is aching.

Day in, day out, nothing changes,
same issues, same faces,
never face any dangers,
my heart ages.

Even my writing is affected tonight,
no passion coming from this crap,
in fact it reads like utter shite,
think I'll call it a wrap.

22nd July
Hey

Hey, what you doing?
Climb a mountain,
swing a cat,
remember to never stop.

Hey, why are you here?
Call me, hold me,
forgive me,
deep breathe in, hold…then release.

Hey, where're you going?
Flight cancelled…again,
dream on,
and so it goes.

Hey, how you been?
Decisions left to chance,
redeem the past,
please don't fall.

Hey, when you leaving?
Gone is gone,
no return,
exciting isn't it.

Hey, what you doing?
Living in riddles,
the code,
too hard to solve.

23rd July
There is a goodness

Close your eyes,
feel the cool breeze,
dance in the darkness,
breathe in the silence,
stretch your sins,
beauty is naked.

Revel in life,
respect its unpredictability,
laugh at its jokes,
cry at its failings,
keep it company,
leave it alone.

There is a goodness,
a reward given out,
as long as you give,
rarely take,
it can read your soul,
decide its present.

Things happen and hurt,
when it's time, it's time,
your beliefs are your own,
as long as you have them,
as long as you are true,
as long as you are you...

...a reflection of who you want to be.

24th July
Just a verse – boss

Meant to be on the sick – my arse,
meant to be ill – whatever,
she's the quality boss – what a farce,
she's the leader – never.

25th July
Come to me

Come to me, talk to me,
sit on my lap and look at me,
you aren't scared are you?
You aren't frightened of little old me?
How could you be?
I have a kind smile
and innocent laugh,
I keep my eyes firmly locked,
watch your every move,
make sure you are safe,
make sure you don't hurt yourself,
make sure you stay near to me,
wouldn't you like that?
Wouldn't you enjoy that?
Wouldn't you want that?
Hear my calming voice,
listen to what I say,
do as you are told,
keep our time together…secret,
keep our time together…precious,
keep our tine together…forever.
Of course you can believe me.
Of course this is normal.
Of course you can trust me I am a…

…teacher.
…vicar.
…TV presenter.
…policeman.
…father.

26th July
Set sail

set sail,
venture out,
open your eyes,
see…

…laugh,
love,
live,
learn…

expand knowledge,
interact,
drench with joy,
be…

…flight,
pure,
broken,
repaired…

revisit people,
reminisce,
stay cool,
we…

…magnetic,
dance,
breathe,
die.

27th July
Roar

There it is in the distance,
revving with anger and spite,
a fury full of penance,
hiding in the dead of night.

It's roar sends you mad,
gives nightmares a voice,
rumbling towards you ironclad,
leaving very little choice.

Frozen to the spot,
the noise consumes your ears,
blood begins to rot,
veins pumping fears.

Face to face you come,
instantly blinding dead eyes,
all functions go numb,
except for screaming cries.

Collapsing in death,
down you go forever,
your final breath,
caused by a drunk driver.

28th July
And so it is

And so it is we cry.

And so it is we kick.

And so it is we grow.

And so it is we learn.

And so it is we fall.

And so it is we rise.

And so it is we taunt.

And so it is we suffer.

And so it is we break.

And so it is we grow up.

And so it is we have fun.

And so it is we are one.

And so it is we find love.

And so it is we work.

And so it is we become slaves.

And so it is we get down.

And so it is we lose sight.

And so it is we make mistakes.

And so it is we bounce back.

And so it is we have faith.

And so it is we fly.

And so it is we spread.

And so it is we bring up.

And so it is we slow down.

And so it is we grow old.

And so it is we look back.

And so it is we smile.

And so it is we die.

And so it is we are never forgotten.

And so it is we are never really dead.

29th July
Hannibal

Blut und Eingeweide, Schweiß und Tränen,
schärfen die Klinge langsam ...,
knie vor dem dunklen Hirsch,
beten für süße Tod
beten für süße Wiedergeburt,
beten für Süße.

Werden Sie das Hauptgericht, Christus geworden,
mit dem Wunsch verschlungen ... eine Leidenschaft,
ein mit der dunklen Hirsch,
Hoffnung für süße Durchgang,
Hoffnung für süße Vergebung,
Hoffnung für Süße.

Das Ritual abgeschlossen, Abendessen getan,
saubere Teller ... aufgebläht,
im Besitz der dunklen Hirsch,
weint über süße Verlust,
weint über süße Verzweiflung,
weinen Süße.

30th July
Shit and sick

Bloody hell,
shit and sick,
wishing well,
feel a dick.

31st July
There was a girl

There was a girl fair and bright,
growing up she shone in the night,
then she met the wrong man,
the sort that did what he can,
abused and tortured every day,
why stay with him, 'why' they say…

…because love is stronger than pain,
rainbows of hope come from rain,
and she felt there was no one else,
and a disease had gripped herself,
but this man decided to abandon her,
causing her strong heart to tear,
and one by one her systems failed,
it's as if they decided to bail,
just as this man had done,
and this horrible disease now won,
and I watched as she died so frail,
everything we did was to a sad avail,
at least peace was now with her,
the memories of him just a blur,
as she shines up the dark night,
this girl once again so fair and bright…

…my mum.

1st August
Maggots

Swarming, crawling...these maggots,
they feed off flesh dark and warm,
blinding my eyes in disgust,
turning my stomach in out, in out.

You blame me, you plague me,
you and yourself bloated,
the fill of me my heritage,
choke on them, choke on me.

In chains, stripped to the bone,
gone is my pride, gone is my resolve,
the stabbing pain of mortality,
coming to a sad bitter end.

And the maggots just move on,
their prejudice limited to 'alive' not 'dead',
the wailing of those left behind,
ignored by those right in front.

2nd August
There is a link

Sky,
music,
coffee,
hair,
light,
breeze,
pain,
mushroom,
head,
Kelly,
stones,
mouse,
thoughts,
cursor,
searching,
bogey,
trapped,
stretch,
calendar,
stand,
anime,
air guitar,
pick away,
scratch head,
Samaritans,
Love or Suicide,
done,
save,
close.

3rd August
This is the way the world ends

I don't want to get shy; don't be shy,
the tick tock tick tock of the wall clock
counting down the many tales,
the bliss of ignorance rides on,
no time to look back in, no time to embrace,
you, me, them; freedom coming to a stop
for this is the way the world ends.

I don't want to get upset; don't be upset,
the chord sounds of existence slows,
now merely a drone in black and white,
whispers of death and loss drift,
their reach passing over all and everything,
you, me, them; waves turning still and silent
for this is the way the world ends.

I don't want to get scared; don't be scared
said the elephant in the room,
for once the future is so very clear,
3 steps away from a grave diggers spade,
and so everything will be forgotten,
you, me, them; abandoned and empty,
for this is the way the world ends.

I don't want to get gone; don't be gone,
surrounded by folded arms,
the silence of time's spectacular death,
I wonder if forgiveness will live on
and lead us out centre stage,
you, me, them; our final slow dance,
for this is the way the world ends.

4th August
Come walk with me

Do you wanna come walk with me?
Do you wanna go for a stroll?
Let's get out of the house,
let's get some fresh air.

Do you wanna come walk with me?
Do you wanna see the sights?
Let's do something away from home,
let's do something away from the TV.

Do you wanna come walk with me?
Do you wanna get some exercise?
Let's communicate as we wander,
let's communicate hand in hand.

Do you wanna come for a walk?
Do you wanna feel the sun?
Let's marvel at the natural world,
let's marvel at the blue sky.

Do you wanna come walk with me?
Do you wanna seem alive?
Let's not forget the beauty,
let's not forget our mortality.

5th August
Half in shadow

Split down the middle,
half in shadow,
half in light,
can you answer this riddle?

Split down the middle,
half in bad,
half in good,
please answer this riddle!

Split down the middle,
half in death,
half in life,
what is the answer to this riddle?

Split down the middle,
half in wrong,
half in right,
is there an answer to this riddle?

Split down the middle,
half in dad,
half in mum,
There is no answer to this riddle!

6th August
eerie or just peaceful

Sat outside having a coffee
with bees flying all around me
loving the lavender plants
watching my cat chasing butterflies!

It really is the simple things
that make it all worthwhile ☺

The only downside
is getting covered in spiders
but getting used to that now
hahaha.

And now a small bug
is inside my laptop screen...

...mind blown!!!

7th August
There is a point

Open your eyes,
there is a point.

Old photographs
of better times,
frozen in glass frames,
half remembered,
half forgotten.

Look back on them,
there was a point.

The 9-5,
a necessary evil
for a good home,
a place of new photographs
and feet up.

Ensure your reservation,
there can be a point.

Growing old,
body and mind failing,
part of the deal,
the privilege of life,
days end drawing near.

Smile into the falling sun,
there's to the point.

8th August
What is that drug?

Hey...you, we're addicted,
sprinkling of this,
a shower of that...
what is that drug?
The one in chocolate.
The one in crisps.
The one in beer.
The one in popcorn.
The one in fizzy drinks...
you know THAT drug!

It takes control of our sanity,
pushes our desire over the edge,
makes us ignore our instincts,
ages already aging bodies,
adds pounds onto pounds onto pounds...
what is that drug?

I need it to help me write.
I need it to help me love.
I need it to help me be better.
I need it to help me expand.
I need it to help me enjoy.

I don't need it to help shorten my life.
I don't need it to help me become docile.
I don't need it to help me spend money I haven't got.
I don't need it to help me develop diseases.
I don't need it to help me die.

So, someone, tell me
what is that drug
and why is it legal?

9th August
As the sun goes down

Amidst a shifting sky
sneaky and cool,
clouds dance and cry
thanks to natures ridicule.

Blades of grass sway
green and bright,
by the distant grey
a subtle hint of night.

A stillness sets in
across beautiful lands,
and peace sparks within
listening to a hearts demands.

So as the sun goes down
and darkness is strewn,
time to pass over the crown
to a brilliant white moon.

10th August
Lazy Sunday

It's a lazy Sunday,
not really a fun day,
more a snooze day,
can't be bothered day,
so what do you say,
are you gonna go my way,
on this lazy Sunday.

11th August
Precious

Frightened skin, thin and old,
black acid pumping cold veins,
a distorted unknown; why me?

Scars need more friends,
the moon pig squeals,
dig, dig, dig for me you fuckers!

Pain is at a loss, so lonely,
fantasies of death re-surface,
carpet burns for my mind.

Into the depths I reside,
my true being trapped complete,
a flick of the coin?

If memory serves falsehood,
actions speak softer than thoughts,
where does my peace lie?

Let's trek through the piss and shit,
live to work to suffer to die,
the oceanic cluster fuck!

What future there is?
Overgrown and garbage,
our blindness celebrated and applauded.

And so we come to the precious,
darkness with a scythe,
hymns of a suicide.

12th August
The mirror has two faces

The sheen of the glass,
don't be fooled!

The world reflected
is a world mirrored,
flatters you not,
speaks no truth,
our mourning of loss.

Inside a blackening,
the same yet somehow
...different.

Who is that staring back?
What are they thinking?
Are they watching you
...when you are not looking?!

Disavowed by those around me,
questioning my own dark reflection,
the mirror has two faces,
the mirror has two places.

This is our last goodbye,
our final cry,
please let us die,
don't ask us why,
the shattered lie.

13th August
Immortality

Fly, fly for me oh sweet beautiful death,
bring with you a bitter and swift end,
for long have I lived and much have I seen,
this immortality has worn out its welcome.

Amongst decayed and derelict concrete,
nature has reclaimed what was once hers,
outlived the arrogance and mortality of humanity,
the bones of which now mere ash; dead dust.

Lion and Tiger no longer caged and put on display.
Whale and Dolphin able to swim in bloodless water.
Monkey and Mouse needed no more for tests.
Cow and Pig fear not of the butchers hook.

The fountains crash, mountains stand tall,
forests dense and alive; radiant,
a fresh air glides through green green grass
and sways with the poppies and blue bells.

The last of my kind, a stranger lost and unwelcome,
my time is well and truly past its use by date
and I cast my tortured mind back to that wish,
a wish for immortality and the want to be the hero...

14th August
World

Drift onwards, drawn by the light.
What is artificial?
What is living?
The heart is bigger on the inside,
the mind is not really caged,
the soul burns forever bright.

Plod through the norm,
give voice to the free,
manipulated we may be
but good at the guessing game,
automatic for the people,
into this mad world we are born.

I vibrate with insanity and loss,
ticking and tocking my time,
going with the flow?
Should be fighting against it!
A smile and a wink,
I'm the best, pick me boss.

And so slipping away,
cellar door shuts behind me
slamming with a knowing nod,
no escape from the bends,
trapped by words and full stops,
three sides to every story they say.

One word.
One chance.
One struggle.
One hope.
One outcome.
One waltz.

15th August
Mortality

And there it is,
a gentle reminder
of our own mortality,
our own fragile moments
on this Earth,
few and far between,
precious time
not to be wasted,
gleefully ignored,
pissed up the wall,
an afterlife of regret,
eternal suffering
and great loss.

16th August
And the reality is...

...people are arseholes.
...animals are uncared for.
...food is expensive.
...life is too short.
...war is profitable.
...imagination is stunted.
...money controls everything.
...we rely on technology.
...governments use fear.
...film is stale.
...originality doesn't exist.
...death is the end.
...humanity will become extinct.
...bridges do burn.
...time does fly.
...
...
...
...
...
...
...
...
...
...

17th August
And the reality is...

Even the strong get weak
the independent become reliant,
the private are exposed
and the young get old.

Nerves die,
muscles wither,
eyes dimmer,
minds lose.

You whole life now limited to a single room
in a house shared with those in the twilight of life,
nothing to do except sit in your favourite chair and doze,
the monotony interrupted by the odd visit by family members.

How does it feel to know death is lingering?
How does it feel to be full of regret?
How does it feel to have lost all faith?
How does it feel to be not very important at all?

Nightmares now come to life,
time rings in your ears,
into the maelstrom you fall,
listening to the last rites.

It's sad.
It's cruel.
It's unfair...

...it's life.

18th August
Back to work

Sing sing back to work we go,
let's hope it doesn't drag go slow,
head up try not to feel too low,
because back to work we will go.

Get in get real get the job done,
no prize though no matter who won,
it's never meant to be fun,
something from you can never run.

And when the day draws to an end,
you haven't been driven round the bend,
time to get out time to send,
your soul begins its mend.

19th August
Whisper (part 1)

Melancholy nights breeze with ease,
their distant worlds living just out of reach
imploring your freedom and love,
deafening with a whisper of true callings.

There is a knot tightened 9 to 5 times,
a necessary evil that trumpets a fanfare
shackles your mind and stumps your nature,
a solitude of pretence drawn out indefinitely.

But remember the melody now repressed,
give it a voice and let it flourish once more,
caged no longer but not without scars,
tears of distended loss and wonder.

20th August
Whisper (part 2)

A wonder reflected in the flickering candle light,
illuminating the prancing shadows and giving life
to the four walls surrounding this lonely writer,
trapped in the shine of the computer screen.

Outside this bubble is a world of encroaching night,
the pitter patter whisper of wildlife coming alive
to witness the distant stars blinking with excitement,
a whole new eco waking up to the smooth darkness.

And in this moment all is right in this odd world,
the love that holds me close burns hard and fast,
a power that keeps me sane and safe; complete,
one of the lucky few, one of the truly thankful.

21st August
Whisper (part 3)

Thankful and in the knowing that there is something
just over there beyond that horizon; tangible,
a wayward dream smouldering in vibrant angst,
bursting with desire across the light fantastic.

The choirs of angels descend through broken clouds,
shimmering shadows follow with rhapsody
chords erupting with emotion and great force,
oh what a sight and sound to behold.

But time weaves its consuming grip and squeezes,
the tightening of that tiny little doubt sneaks in
and forms a crack from within the black,
what was once a whisper now begins its torment.

22nd August
Whisper – (epilogue)

When the torment takes hold,
hatred grows
inside,
slowly infecting the goodness,
purging out feelings of hope
entertaining thoughts of suicide,
remembrance in those melancholy nights.

23rd August
I walk with the dead

Blinded by my surroundings,
I walk with the dead,
bodies lay motionless
on my journey,
round and round in circles,
I fear I am next,
I fear my time is up,
I fear…fear.

Then I am lifted higher,
taken to an escape
and set free on the wind,
let me go home,
oh please let me be,
guide me back,
guide me away,
guide…guide me.

"I do not know whatever happened
to the one I set free on the wind,
I only wish he made his way home,
I only wish I can make my back home"

24th August
It only takes one sentence

Be true to who you are
and pass judgement on that person,
and that person alone.

25th August
Bank Holiday Monday

YIPPEE!!!!!

26th August
Skin on skin

The anticipation is consuming me
taking over any rationality and sense,
who said fantasies should stay fantasies?
Skin on skin...let's begin!

That first touch is speechless,
no turning back,
lips quiver and dry up,
our sex is needed,
our desires acted out.

Clothes slide off in a heap,
our bodies mirrored
as we explore and dance,
kiss and join,
hard and soft,
this is serious!

Heating up we entwine,
wanting all and everything,
time has no power here,
time has no meaning,
tasting each other,
wetting our appetites,
salty and sweet,
hot and sticky.

It doesn't matter who we are.
It doesn't matter our gender.
It doesn't matter our relationship.
It doesn't matter the reasons.
What matters is our consent.
What matters is our passion.
What matters is our freedom.
What matters is our skin on skin.

27th August
Work

It's hard,
but not impossible.
It's a pain,
but not painful.
It's frustrating,
but not hurtful.
It's harsh,
but not wounding.
It's…work.

28th August
Farewell

It's funny. We moved out of 68 Cornbrook at the start of May but it has still felt like my home; my house. Even though we are now pretty much settled in Halsall (after a rough start) and have it virtually the way we want it, there was still that part of me living in Cornbrook.

Maybe it was because I lived there for 37 years. Maybe it was because I spent years on my own. Maybe it was because we were the same. Big on the outside, empty on the inside. Neglected, falling apart, cold, abandoned, lost...old.

In the end I couldn't wait to get out of there and then immediately began to miss it. I don't think I ever got chance to say a proper goodbye due to the absolute nightmare of moving on that last day which could also account for feeling like it was still my home.

Today, I have just seen photos online of it completed and refurbished and it looks stunning! It doesn't even look like the same house...it looks...young again. A good family will look after it and breathe new life into it, give its heart a reason to beat again.

And yet, I feel...sad. Almost like I have lost a friend; a true friend. One that kept me safe and warm, one that was always there for me no matter what, one that listened, never judged, witnessed horrible acts, experienced wrong things...a survivor.

68 Cornbrook is no longer my home. 68 Cornbrook is no longer my house. 68 Cornbrook is no longer the friend I had. 68 Cornbrook will live in my memories now forever. 68 Cornbrook will remain a part of my life we both survived. 68 Cornbrook will no doubt be waiting for me regardless of where I end up when I die, whether it be Heaven or Hell, it will be there protecting me and loving me...God bless 68 Cornbrook – farewell.

29th August
Re-spect

Re-spect,
walk,
prick,
bleed,
broken,
glass,
alone,
planet,
insane,
hostile,
cemetery,
cowboys!!!

30th August
Senses numb

When you've seen
what I have seen,
heard those words
that should never be spoken,
lived and died
a million times,
over and over,
senses numb.

There is no originality,
humanity is heading to hell,
right and wrong are farce,
we live in a fantasy world,
our beings forced into it,
this poem means nothing,
our eventuality is set.

All questions...answered,
all music...heard,
all words...read,
all stories...told,
all feelings...felt,
all porn...seen,
all notions...rectified,
all time...lost.

The prisons that keep us dogs,
designed to comfort instead of hold,
trick our souls into believing free will,
constantly breaking then rebuilding
our hearts...our minds...our individuality,
senses numb...senses numb...senses numb.

31st August
an old friend

I went to see an old friend today,
with a face a new and a body to boot,
yet deep down inside this old friend,
was the same one I left back in May.

The insides had been gutted away,
all new parts to give him strength,
the will of the young renewed and bright,
a brand new house some might say.

Yet underneath the makeover and clay,
my old friend so dear to me smiled
and remains mine no matter what,
tethered together forever and a day.

1st September
Where am I?

Dawning of a new year,
months into two zero one four,
what is this, where am I?

Settled? More so.
Happy? Never truly.
Alive? Unknown.
Suicidal? Buried…for now.

The loneliness hits me
like debris in space,
sometime battered,
sometimes scraped…
always there.

A forever void consumes my sexuality,
drags me this way then the next,
the fire that burns the hottest
doesn't care what it burns
and doesn't mind what ignites it.

And then comes the war,
raging in time, raging in blind,
this constant struggle,
an autopsy for yin and yang
played out in the eyes,
spilling,
infecting,
winning…
losing.

So I ask where am I?
And I answer…
same place I have always been.

2nd September
Evil

It seeks, creeps,
dances with the dead,
dirties innocent hands,
a rift of diseased blood
and black acid...burning,
suffocating and consuming,
a haven in plain view.

Its greatest victory,
the influence of dark whispers
chipping away hope and light,
condemning the good
and breathing poison,
a masterpiece of influence,
a marvel of conflict...

...the infected questioning,
how could I have become this?
I have a pure heart,
a clever mind,
a bright future...
how could I have become this?

Evil is what makes,
it lives in us all,
it has to be in us all,
it needs to desire in us all...
why?

So we can see the good.
So we can do the good.
So we can be the good.

3rd September
Coldness of the keyboard

Look at its drab colour,
letters and numbers proud,
cleanly outlined with perfection,
clinical and sort of square,
the coldness of a keyboard.

Blinking lights,
a squidgy screen,
bouncy keys,
a warm bottom,
wires extruding,
the grey case,
stickers advertising,
indent identity,
a slight hum,
the always watching eye,
rubber stoppers,
holes for memory stuff,
impersonal,
cheap,
nasty...

...yet...

...inside lives a world,
no – a million worlds.

The works and imagination
of the creative few thrive,
every sentence beats
with a pulse so strong,
so vibrant and glorious
that is has the power to move,
the power to inspire,
the power to live.

4th September
Dare to…

…inspire.

5th September
In

In it goes,
slowly at first...

...the burning sensation
sends shivers up your spine,
catches your breath
as out it comes.

In it goes,
with meaning this time...

...the strange sensation
sends wild thoughts in your mind,
biting your lip
as out it comes.

In it goes,
filling you up completely...

...the glorious sensation
sends you into a riding frenzy,
closing your eyes
as out it comes.

In it goes...

...this time it goes in and out and in and out and in and out,
hitting that spot over and over and over again,
fucking you any which way it wants,
for however long it wants...until,
it comes.

6th September
In the dark

Writing...in the dark.
Music...in the dark.
Horny...in the dark.
Drinking...in the dark.
Watching...in the dark.
Thoughts...in the dark.
Living...in the dark.
Peace...in the dark.
Ghost...in the dark.
Devin...in the dark.
Gushing...in the dark.
Sharing...in the dark.
Moonlight...in the dark.
Breeze...in the dark.
Disturbing...in the dark.
Shadows...in the dark.
Glowing...in the dark.
Tinkering...in the dark.
Full up...in the dark.
Erotic...in the dark.
Fucked...in the dark.
Fantasy...in the dark.
Dreaming...in the dark.
Desire...in the dark.
Spread...in the dark.
Alone...in the dark.
Alone...in the dark.
Alone...in the dark.

7th September
Surrounded by beauty

The sky is blue.
The grass is green.
The sun is yellow.
The clouds are white.
The breeze is cool.
The air is fresh.
The feeling is warm.
The silence is golden.

Everywhere I look,
I am surrounded by beauty,
distant trees march,
far away hills roll,
fields of hay sway...

(ducks quack,
chickens cluck,
cows moo,
bees buzz)

...never will it be said that I am not lucky,
never will it be said that I suffer,
never will it be said that I struggle,
never will it be said that I made the wrong choice.

The state of the world in 2014 disgusts me,
suffering, power and greed rule over all,
men, women and children simply exist,
their lives based on pure survival...
nothing more...nothing less.

8th September
Twinkle twinkle…

Blackness boils with sweetness,
liquid hatred brimming; swimming
as sliced wrists dry up and stiffen,
the twinkle twinkle spark now gone.

Rainbows of dark and light travel
inheriting the souls of the damned,
a claw finger of desperation; fear
captures the spirit with intent,
intent to rape and destroy,
intent to inflict and burn,
intent to suffer and sacrifice.

And a lonely chord sings,
straining with loss and anger,
fuelling the demons desire
and increasing the wealth of torture,
a fine art indeed; this masterpiece,
changing with the seasons of hell,
twisting to its keepers will,
eternal with its execution.

There will be blood.
There will be pain.
There will be regret.
There will be cruelty.

There will be no remorse.
There will be no pity.
There will be no hope.
There will be no end.

9th September
Little star…

Your light has gone out
extinguished by your own sins,
the devils dance a macabre
of irony and charm.

Slowly you begin to rot
from the inside out,
blind with terror,
blind with scarring.

Little star now gone,
no prick of white left,
huddled in a heap of ash,
discarded on a whimsy.

Judgement of self,
only what you deserve,
a cradle of filth
to send you to sleep…

…no remorse,
no pity,
no hope,
no end.

10th September
Innocence

The older we get,
the more we lose,
the wiser we become,
the dumber we are.

When innocence fades
and age takes over,
imagination turns to stone
and wonder becomes fact.

Can you remember:

the last time you rolled about in the grass
the last time you coloured in a picture
the last time you laughed at the sky
the last time you were amazed at trees
the last time you pointed towards the moon
the last time you dreamt of magic
the last time you grazed your knee
the last time you ran after the ice cream man?

Now you are all serious,
working yourself to an early grave.

Now you are all grown up,
angry and moaning till dark.

Now you are all sad,
childhood happiness long gone.

Wouldn't it be nice to regain some of that innocence?!?!?!?!?

11th September
Underappreciated

Do you ever get the feeling
that you are fucking underappreciated?
Get the feeling that there is
a very solid lack of support?

Instead of criticism,
instead of nagging,
instead of picking,
instead of listening…

…I know, lets underappreciate,
let's say the most unhelpful thing,
let's kick a man when he is down,
let's do the opposite of what should be done.

Sounds like a good idea,
sounds like I should ignore
the desire to think
before I speak.

Fuck it.
Fuck it.
Fuck it.
Fuck it.

12th September
Dare to…

…remember.

13th September
There are some people…

…born into this world with no meaning,
part of this planet with no reason.

Those who are pure scum,
no concept of right and wrong,
loud and "look at me pathetic",
always have to go one better,
always have to buy one bigger,
always have to be known to all.

They have money but don't work.
They have children but don't parent.
They have holidays but don't save.
They have rules but don't follow.

Criminals,
disloyal,
two faced,
abusive,
idiotic,
leeches,
fucking scum fuckers.

But we need them,
so the rest of us
have a low to measure against,
we need them
so the rest of us
can strive to be better,
kinder,
more honest,
important.

14th September
Build a wall

Line the path,
line the tracks,
build a wall,
encase the fire.

Lead the way,
lead the route,
build a wall,
encase the land.

Load the footing,
load the square,
build a wall,
encase the ownership.

Like the job,
like the effort,
build a wall,
encase the life.

Leave the end,
leave the pain,
build a wall,
encase the past.

Last the man,
last the name,
build a wall,
encase the future.

15th September mess

early up,
not much sleep,
dodgy tummy,
swimming in air,
off to work; Porsche,
drive faster,
gonna be one of those days,

stupid issues,
angry head,
why do we bother?
calms down,
bit more relaxed,
get on with it,
meeting followed by...

...meeting – then dinner,

coffee comes next,
yummy and warm,
almost home time,
then a final flourish,
a final puzzle,
sorted,
bit of overtime,
home time,

drive fast (not that fast though),
home, dinner on, take off uniform,
talk, listen, eat, shit...

...write, write, write, mess.

16th September
Mac and Kennedy…

make
me
feel
young
again…

make
me
feel
happy
again…

make
me
feel
wonder
again…

make
me
feel
laughter
again…

make
me
feel
free
again.

17th September
Work and Sanko…

make
me
feel
old
again…

make
me
feel
useless
again…

make
me
feel
unwanted
again…

make
me
feel
hatred
again…

make
me
feel
trapped
again.

18th September
Inception

Laughter and fun,
building our own worlds
with the simplest of ideas,
a paradox of stubbornness
and dark pride.

It clouds and suffocates
the basic human need,
collapsing the dream,
old souls full of regret,
a casualty of past blackness.

"The family name must not go on,
the blood line must stop here,
no farther, no more, no suffering...

...this self-inflicted punishment defies sense,
an inception of pain and dirt,
I am not what I fear I could be."

Through the eyes and thoughts
of Mac and Kennedy I fly,
the person I should be and not he,
my time a reflection of loss
in bitterness and sadness,
for may the passing on to child
give rise to a new spark,
conditions and actions of never,
never, never, never, never...

...now, consideration.

19th September
A quick hello

Doesn't take much,
a quick hello,
bit of respect,
bit of interaction.

Doesn't require a lot,
a small acknowledgment,
nod of the head,
little wave.

Doesn't eat energy,
a tiny effort,
nice gesture,
friendly manner.

But to be ignored,
a big action,
not very nice,
not very respectful.

But to be blanked,
a conscience decision,
no need,
no explanation.

But to be disrespected,
a grave mistake,
what goes around,
will definitely come around.

20th September
Hell = Earth

Hell – the place of the dead in general:
aren't we all born to die?
the abode of evil spirits:
isn't the planet full of them?
any place of vice or misery:
humanity suffers constantly.
a place of turmoil:
beheadings, rape, paedophilia.
anything causing pain or destruction:
wars, bombings, genocide.
ruin, havoc, commotion, uproar:
death of forests, pillaging, riots.

Hell = Earth.
Fact.

You tell me.
Watch the news.
Read a paper.
Live.

Hell = Earth?
Hell = Earth!

21st September
Dare to…

[redacted]

…move out of the darkness.

22nd September
The shimmering sky

There is a layer of red,
a cushion of blue,
the shimmering sky,
reflects me and you.

Greens and browns,
flood the horizon,
sounds of nature,
singing to the sun.

And when the night comes,
a stillness it brings,
stars twinkle and shine,
thrones of kings.

A very lucky man I am,
after all I've been through,
a reward of such it must be,
but a reward from who?

23rd September
A foreboding

Eerie fog drifts on the horizon,
Godspeed within the devils thunder
surrounded by the imminent of hell,
a fairy-tale of twisted nails,
laugh, laugh, laugh; madness comes.

A falling star...this foreboding
bringing with it the ultimate sorrow,
the death of love; lost and black,
leaving nothing but disdain and hate,
laugh, laugh, laugh; madness comes.

Evil swims across this open land,
now a tragic kingdom of blissful suffering
as walking corpses rape and cannibalise,
no more shadows, no more light,
laugh, laugh, laugh: madness comes.

Dusk brings with it a flame of sulphur,
sweet and deadly; without prejudice,
a taste of cruelty and the beast
consuming all that stand in its way,
laugh, laugh, laugh; madness comes.

And the bones of the Earth crumble,
floating on a wind of screams at midnight,
this is darkness incarnate; purity
taken to a bitter and sad end,
laugh, laugh, laugh; madness comes.

Silence,
stillness,
peace,
nothing,
madness.

24th September
Missed moments

The lost opportunities, the missed moments,
a forward glance caught backwards,
the wrong answer to the right question,
can I sit next to you?

Good byes never said, passing strangers,
forgotten deeds long gone,
misunderstood words said with pain,
can I make it up to you?

All the bells and all the whistles,
material surroundings decay,
act with those that matter the most,
can I play out with you?

We waste and consume, fear and shrink,
our little legs barely carrying us over,
a puppet losing its strings,
can I draw strength from you?

And from the hand of death comes regret,
too late to want more time,
the gift of which only now burns,
can I wait for you?

25th September
There were trumpets

Suddenly there was a thief,
dancing to the rhythm
busting a move; gratuitous.

Directions needed for practice,
point this way then that,
I was ready, are you ready?

Thunder erupts inside,
questioning everybody's anger,
a bands strength; weakness.

Happy together as one,
myself walking hand in hand,
forever married to me.

Laugh, laugh, laugh; madness,
thrown off only to get back on,
gotta keep them riding.

I just want to go home,
cross the streets with safety,
please baby, sing me a chorus.

Hold, hold, hold; madness,
how can I be very important?
too many mixed signals.

Crack a mirror, smile a joke,
those beautiful girls,
shacked up with the richness.

Brutha this and homey that,
surrounded by concrete,
old school peeps; what's that noise...

...there were trumpets.

26th September
Written in the future about the past trilogy That feeling

Coming to the end,
that feeling,
the shit now behind,
the piss now done,
as time ticks away,
eats its fill for the week,
fit to burst, fit to implode.

Blind freedom,
that feeling,
the routine to follow,
as strict now as before,
rules always there,
forcing them to be followed,
don't deviate, don't dare.

Surrounded by things,
that feeling,
filling the spaces,
blocking up the hole,
money will be wasted,
but a need to want more,
its power, its evil.

Memories of youth,
that feeling,
every day was new,
an adventure just waiting,
age is the death of us all,
the one thing we share,
no exception, no escape.

27th September Written in the future about the past trilogy When I was young

I had imagination,
a wonder so bright,
deep passion for play,
energy that last forever,
the world completely open,
everything free,
a big sing along.

Questions unanswered,
amazement in cars,
lost in cartoons,
journeys in the garden,
adventures in the mind,
everything new,
a big sing along.

Emotions flooding,
interest in the opposite sex,
friends that fly,
grandparents that read,
music of passion,
everything exciting,
a big sing along.

When I was young,
pain hid in mirrors,
a broken Mother cried,
an abusive Father lied,
hatred saturated the walls,
bled from injustice,
everything wrong,
a big sing along.

28th September
Written in the future about the past trilogy
Ladies and gentlemen we are floating in space

Cracked mirrors turn to dust,
the disease trapped inside floats away
and the inevitability of "right"
overshadows the "wrong",
these souls of fate and destiny collide,
their worlds apart now as one,
ladies and gentlemen we are floating in space.

Ruling the world or not,
together they are no matter how far
as raised voices always lead to soft words,
a turned back ending with a strong embrace
because amidst the shit and piss is love,
pure, simple, powerful love,
ladies and gentlemen we are floating in space.

Then there is that feeling,
the connection impossible to break,
like painting in the dark
or swimming in the sun,
hand in hand through fire and tar,
footprints on the ceiling,
ladies and gentlemen we are floating in space.

And so it comes to the end,
the outcome of all good things,
written in the future about the past,
yet what goes around comes around,
every up has its down,
every yes has it's no…and remember
ladies and gentlemen, we are floating in space.

29th September
Slender man

Tall, thin, distant, bright,
Slender man comes a visiting,
creeping through the darkness,
reaching through the night.

His blank suit a pierce,
his long arms growing,
his slate like face stares,
his relentless pursuit is fierce.

Messages of chalk warn,
screams of the lost suffer,
children snatched and dead,
families left completely torn.

There is no running away,
there is no turning back,
there is no help coming,
there is no nothing to say.

Tall, thin, distant, bright,
Slender man is already here,
hiding in the darkness,
living in the night.

30th September
Dare to…

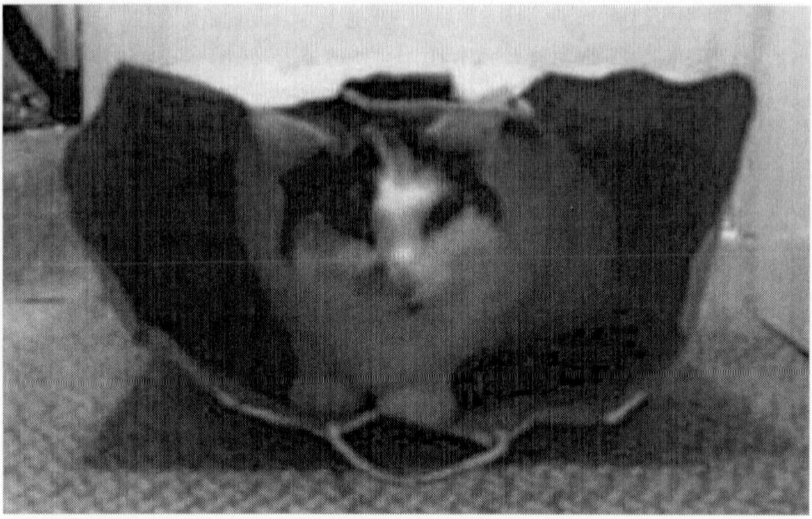

....cat in a bag??

1st October
all you need is six lines
part 1

let's not emphasise the detail,
instead bring all the sins of emotion,
because all you need is six lines
to dig through the piss and shit,
six lines bleeding with hurt and pain,
six lines breathing with life and death.

2nd October
all you need is six lines
part 2

one,
two,
three,
four,
five,
six, six, six.

3rd October
all you need is six lines
part 3

and so the daily slog continues,
banging your head against the brick wall.

and so the daily slog continues,
the lack of achievement and appreciation the norm.

and so the daily slog continues,
no importance in what we do, no contribution to humanity.

4th October
all you need is six lines
part 4

82 days to go...

...Lancaster here we come...

...a set of eye pieces...

...to see far into space...

...expand her imagination...

...make her go wow.

5th October
all you need is six lines
part 5

There are instances when I look out across
the horizon and stop.
Moments in time when I sit and listen;
come to a very real conclusion.
Watching fireworks explode and light up
the night sky with glee.
Nothing but silence and beauty surrounding
all of my little thoughts.
And remembering where I have been, where
I was and where I am now.
I am one very, very, very, very lucky son of
a bitch...and I know it.

6th October
all you need is six lines
part 6

six has been and always will be my lucky number,
this is part 6 of all you need is six lines,
Queen's sixth album was the first album I heard by them,
'F' is the sixth letter; 'F' is for food and fanny,
today is the 6th October and I am off work,
666 is the number of the beast.

7th October
all you need is six lines
part 7

Light the candle.

Sit back and remember.

Think about your past, present and future.

Good times, bad times, proud moments and regrets.

Things you have done, things you have seen, things you have said.

Do you weep? Do you smile? Do you feel empty? Do you feel full? Do you?

8th October
all you need is six lines
part 8

A shared desire between the eyes of the sinful,
the feeling deep inside of wanton pleasure,
to hell with the little voices telling you it's wrong
because this passion is unstoppable,
this raw, powerful passion is madness purified,
a shift capable of breaking hearts and destroying lives.

9th October
all you need is six lines
part 9

Knife like rain batters down all around
as tumbling grey clouds roll like mountains,
an air of stagnation creeps and crawls
seeping into the very pores of life itself,
the only hope is seen in the distance,
a single ray of light cutting through the gloom.

10th October
all you need is six lines
part 10

and so the week comes to an end; end?

the bastard week of the bastard son; sanko?

not much done, little time spent out; away?

realities of the power money has over us; God?

yet wandering thoughts leave words of desire; crazy?

things set in motion leading to a path travelled not; passion?

11th October
all you need is six lines
part 11

There is a hole in the wall
where the creatures can get in,
a hole in the wall
open to the elements,
but this hole in the wall
is nothing more than a sunset.

12th October
all you need is six lines
part 12

what is the purpose of my life? here I am.

will I die suddenly, will I die painfully,
will I die heroically? a wish.

a pale communion awaits or a dark
mourning flounders? this test.

am I to be remembered with love, am
I to be remembered with hate? fear.

welcomed as a lamb of God, rejected
as a driver of Satan? fallen.

is it all just a guessing game with a big
black nothingness at the end? probably.

<u>13th October
all you need is six lines
part 13</u>

give me your sex,

allow me the urge,

let me taste your insides out,

get lost in your body, mind and soul…the euphoric passion draining our desire,

heat, power, fulfilment, pure, naughty, strong…

…fucking.

14th October
all you need is six lines
part 14

There is such a goodness, a cathedral of hope and smiles,
yet the scars scream 'please don't touch'.

An honour and pride burning through the piss and shit,
merely a front hiding the disappointment and hatred within.

Strength to lead with love and the energy of the young,
my little voice shaking in the darkness; scared, lost, dead.

15th October
all you need is six lines
part 15

Is this all a dream,
a reality of fantasy and make-believe?
Are we really here,
living, breathing, loving, hating, suffering?
Or does the world disappear,
everything vanish when you close your eyes?

16th October all you need is six lines part 16

loneliness

solitude

hatred

pain

slice

goodnight, goodnight.

17th October all you need is six lines part 17

Listen to the thickness abound,
be blown away by the deep sound,
it pins your heart to the ground,
as the vinyl spins round and round,
and the love of music is re-found,
wrapped on its little finger I am wound.

18th October
all you need is six lines
part 18

tip toe through the moments in time unique and bizarre
for the mundane attempts to control and dominate.

be wary of technology replacing those around you
because flesh and blood cannot be re-booted if it dies.

who you are is who you are and as long as there is a goodness
there will be those who will bring you down to their level.

19th October
all you need is six lines
part 19

6. six slices to make; cake or skin
5. five digits to make a fist; what do you do
4. four limbs to do as we please; hurt or help
3. three dimensions to wander; in or out
2. two hearts; one broken, one fixed
1. one soul; in this life

20th October
all you need is six lines
part 20

The sickness inside gives me a little kick
to let me know he's still there,
the disturbances in my sleep pattern
and waking up soaked all but confirm,
feeling down and worthless in work is a
return to form for that little voice,
"I am a fat waste of piece of shit space"
and I am never to forget that fact,
repeat those words with no escape and
no freedom from the father inside me,
"I hope you make the same mistake"
destined to haunt my existence forever.

21st October
all you need is six lines
part 21

Never forget the ones you love,
these are the ones who love you,
the ones who accept you,
the ones who live with you,
the ones who laugh with you,
the ones who cry with you...

22nd October
all you need is six lines
part 22

...when you open your eyes in the morning, there they are,
when you go to bed at night, it's their arms wrapped around you,
when you talk about the absolute mundane,
they are the ones who listen,
when you are beaten down by the world around,
they pick you up...

...you don't need to impress the ones you love,
you don't need to pretend to the ones who love you.

23rd October
all you need is six lines
part 23

Time to rest, time to sleep...the city is on fire,
stop looking at dirty pictures old man...hell awaits,
the darkness erupts into suffocation...an afterglow,
creamy? bitter? sweet? goes down so well...sipping,
and the words come flooding from a place unknown...far away,
drifting into dreams and nightmares...shared as one.

24th October
all you need is six lines
part 24

The returning gaps...

sleepless and disturbed, waking dreamlike moments; what? minutes seem like hours, tossing and turning – the slightest sound.

Am I heading down that road again? The beginning of the end? Has the puppet master regained his control...re-attached his strings...

...am I being played with, toyed with, brought to my knees once again?

25th October
all you need is six lines
part 25

hot
sexy
tasty
wet
come
been a while!

26th October
all you need is six lines
part 26

Why would you live in a world you aren't able to change?
Constantly complaining about the wrong doings
aimed directly at you
and blaming anything and everything other than yourself.

You look above your head every day and see the strings,
faulting them for your mistakes, regrets and pathetic worries...

...but ask yourself; who is the real puppet and who
is the real master?

27th October
all you need is six lines
part 27

The return of an alien hell bent on Earths destruction,
fuelled by coffee and brother of the spectacular captain,
scored by choirs and magnificent bombastic foolishness.

Then we find ourselves floating in the blue sky; soaring,
passing the midnight sun into a rain city; forever,
never forget the ones we love; never forget.

28th October
all you need is six lines
part 28

I am not a good man, I am not a worthy man,
I am not a good boyfriend, I am not a good brother,
I was not a good son, I am not a good son.

I could be so much more.
I could do so much more.
I should have protected her more.

29th October
all you need is six lines
part 29

Grind, eyes locked, bodies joined,
being controlled and trapped,
a violent kiss demands intention
as skin heats up and insides joy,
the world seems so very far away,
the here and now pure fucking.

30th October
all you need is six lines
part 30

It rests its hands over my shoulders,
taps me on the head as a gentle nudge.

Appears in the corner of the mirror,
stepping on that one creaky floor board.

Burning my mind and thoughts with ease,
reminding me how worthless and useless I am.

31st October
all you need is six lines
part 31

so did I emphasise the detail?
did I bring all the sins of emotion?
do you need more than six lines
to dig through the piss and shit,
six lines bleeding with hurt and pain,
six lines breathing with life and death...did I?

1st November
Questions

Don't dare question what you are not willing to change,
your thin honour wants to be part of this world
but it isn't willing to help it; a stab in the back.

Ignoring the suffering,
complaining about the lack of luxury
in your world of comfort,
not even realising the strings...

...black, infinite, unbreakable.

The endless cycle of hushed tones,
guessing this and that,
putting too much faith in stories,
putting too much faith in words,
putting too much faith in men.

And so you end up running away from you
instead of facing the piss and shit.
You end up accepting the strings dangling
with swaying menace and control.
Watching innocence pay the price,
listening to the wrong answers
and mourning the wrong people...

...universal hope is never too far away.

Can you set yourself free?
Can you cut the strings?
Can you?

2nd November
Grace of Innocence

With the grace of innocence
the slightest of touches screams,
swimming in endless possibilities
and realms of heated desire.

A few words said in passing
hinting at something much more,
the meaning not yet fully clear,
the outcome not yet fully realised.

Passionate eyes locked in place
for a moment that shouts forever,
drawn to each other with fallout,
destiny and fate having a little bit of fun.

Yet that barrier remains intact and strong,
the only defence between bloody kisses,
for how long though no one knows,
the burning flame of pure magnet lust.

3rd November
Breath

Shivering excitement,
wild thoughts,
a hint of wrongfulness...

...or maybe a load of naughtiness?

The possibilities emanating from her body,
exploring every curve, every line, every last inch,
touch...and taste; forbidden fruit.

Her lips demanding heat,
her neck exposed and pale; vulnerable,
her heart beating fast and hard,
her stomach full of electricity,
her insides wet to the touch; magnetic,
her legs taut, feet reaching...

...her being wanting and desiring,
passion on her breath,
desire on her mind,
the world in her eyes,
control in her actions; you are not you,
you are hers...now...and forever.

4th November
Away

Sometimes I just want to be away,
flying high above with my Mother,
safe in her arms,
trapped in her smile,
comforted in her warmth.

Singing together,
our minds locked,
the past forgiven,
the future ours...

...hey, are you afraid,
to say what you are
trying to say.

Sometimes I just want to be away,
sweet revenge on my Father,
breaking his arms,
pounding his smile,
robbing him of his warmth.

Damned together,
our minds warped,
the past never forgotten,
the future non-existent...

...hey, are you afraid,
to say what you are
trying to say...

...hey, are you afraid,
to say what you are
trying to say.

5th November Around

To be part of the interaction
between Mother and children,
to be amongst the love
between blood and soul.

As the fireworks fly,
the sparklers dance,
the night lights up
and the air softens.

Memories of days long gone
flood through the laughter,
memories of days long forgotten
now a casualty of harsh reality.

Laughter and fun,
wonder and imagination,
innocence and youth,
a disco for the ants.

And after the invite inside reveals much more,
an admiration and respect deepens,
a simple thought voiced; expressed,
"I couldn't do that".

6th November
Random

5:15am,
life story,
sleep…not for long,
lights on,
shower,
slow…wondering if?

The drive down Plex Moss Lane,
through Lydiate and Maghull,
onto the Motorway and onwards,
onwards to work…work…work.

Typing,
meetings,
8D's,
knowing a new face,
knowing an old face,
Dan-san.

The usual slog of the 8:30-5:00,
could be much worse,
could be much better,
onwards to the end of the day.

Yet grumble we mustn't,
as rape and murder this is not,
it's just a damn job,
pays the bills.

It's shopping time,
its pizza time,
its writing time,
its Ziltoid time!!!!

7th November
saucerful

Menacing vibrations
eerie and dark,
creeping plinks and plonks,
their air of strain encompassing.

A drone inside my head
switches moods; swinging madness,
danger, danger...flashing pain
and a whimpering paleness lost and sharp.

Is it this way or is it that way?
the noise clasps my head with vice claws
screeching down my throat,
there is nowhere to run
from the beating,
from the drumming failure
that emanates from my whole being.

Wavering limbs crumble,
the piano lid comes down
crashing and crushing,
slice after slice after slice...

...and the carpet stains red.

But for this, a sense of peace rumbles in,
a lone chord plays out like a funeral march
as complete loneliness settles over quiet death,
(no more secrets left)
my path now set by a procession...on and on,
the world drifts away...going, going, gone,
angels morn the victory of my weakness and weep,
reaching as my soul is dragged downwards,
the glee of suicide has claimed another,
the sadness of despair has won...

8th November
Interstellar/Cuckoo

Settled dust upon a weary soul,
the fantasy of possibilities dry and cracked,
wanton dreams evaporated long ago,
memories of the last dance a dim thought
stretched out thin and sore; tearful.

A figure in the rain calls me on,
her hair blowing in the crisp wind,
her body silhouetted by the fading light,
muffled urgency in her voice is lost
forever taken from me; banished.

And my head drops in defeat,
no-one to hear my final words,
no-one to see my last smile,
my life nothing but a whisper in the night,
an echo of failure and blood; cuckoo.

9th November
Essence inside me (part 1) – just the beginning

Mesmerised by the dark air in the room
my s[redacted]are flooded with new [redacted]bilities,
[redacted]w demanding to [redacted]
[redacted]fucked in eve[redacted]

[redacted]g my[redacted]
[redacted]
th[redacted]sire.

Touc[redacted]nning,
a shive[redacted]pties me
[redacted]
my be[redacted]me first.

Using the sa[redacted]haft on shaft,
our [redacted]aving
whils[redacted]in skin
[redacted]of fi[redacted]

[redacted]ps me to my[redacted]y,
[redacted]nsuming every la[redacted]h
slid[redacted]den lips over this pro[redacted]mber,
dripping spit landing on my own [redacted]erce coc[redacted].

[redacted]
wa[redacted]ng as he guides himself in by grabbing my[redacted]ist,
no escape [redacted]s I feel my insides slide over with wanton[redacted]pleasure…

10th November
Essence inside me (part 2) – down to business

...rampant and relentless
my ass [illegible] d hard
[illegible]

[illegible]

h[illegible]k
with a de[illegible]nd joyful.

With a swift[illegible]nto my back,
my legs sprea[illegible]and sideways,
I grab them[illegible]exhilaration
as h[illegible]ase,
m[illegible]ng
as fast[illegible]d heat.

[illegible]

11th November
Essence inside me (part 3) – becoming serious

…this is now becoming serious. Our innocent play is gone as I stare at this [redacted] say, [redacted]

[redacted] his [redacted] of [redacted] and [redacted]

We [redacted] as I [redacted] out [redacted] on [redacted] of [redacted] He [redacted] as I [redacted]

I [redacted] and [redacted] and [redacted] to [redacted] he has [redacted] his [redacted] of warmth deep inside and [redacted] stroke as he empties himself completely. His eyes [redacted] body is rumbling and his [redacted]

As I begin sucking, licking [redacted] of our session, he grabs the back of my head [redacted] his cock regaining its full strength as I [redacted] of my mouth over my body with one hand and [redacted] anus with the other. This isn't finished. This isn't over. [redacted] the beginning.

12th November
worn out

Ever written something so taboo and passionate...

...it has worn you out and is actually just too much!!!

[redacted]

yes......

[redacted]

13th November
That feeling

Twisting knots,
excited and dangerous,
the enticement,
the happy dread,
the anticipation.

That feeling;
you know the one,
horny and wicked,
desirable and wild,
touching yourself
uncontrollably,
vividly.

Letting the imagination loose,
fantasies wanting to be explored,
prohibitions demanding to be released,
who really cares about rules?
Who really cares about being normal?

Limits are meant to be pushed,
lines are supposed to be stepped over,
life is only lived once…so live it.

14th November
torn

"The fall of a good man is worth more to the devil
than the evil nature of a bad man"

There is a definitive split,
a rip between myself and me,
an outside façade
well respected and decent,
an inside desire
completely twisted and wild.

I want to be explored.
I want to be loved.
I want to be here.
I want to be gone.
I want to go too far.
I want to be respectful.
I want to believe in Heaven.
I want to go to Hell.
I want to destroy the world.
I want save us all.
I want to be torn.
I want to be whole.

And there will come a time when my strength will fail,
a time when I will lose everything and everyone
in search of the taboo; the forbidden passion.
And when this time comes,
my Father's words will ring true,
"Hope this happens to you one day".

15th November
connect

Push the boundaries,
create that profile,
set out your goals,
post your first post,
like and repost,
begin the connection,
get followers,
follow followers,
build up a folio,
get intimate,
get real,
message,
reply,
fantasies shared,
fantasies explored,
reveal all,
take it further,
meet up,
get fucked,
be fucked,
do the fucking,
move on,
rinse and repeat...

...two zero one four,
humanities interaction.

16th November
Random-ness

marching, waiting,
flying,

scratching...coffee.

Numb head, cold toes,
prepare for the count down,
stretching with clenched fists,
admiring the landscape,
imaging the taboo...
...essence inside me.

Stubble...sweet female voice serenades,
watching, waiting,
need money to buy toys,
special toys...yum yum,
shot at again...sing it loud,
sing it loud, sing it loud.

Spinning ideas rushing through my head,
desires and passions wanting to be fulfilled,
tearing my standards and loyalty apart,
yet the voices screaming their orders,
orders I cannot and must not ignore...

...random-ness.

17th November
In the darkness

In the darkness we live,
our dirty little secrets
purged of all exposure,
our wanton desires
prancing free,
our passionate thoughts
caged no more.

Whispering,
clothes peeled off,
a little laugh,
echoing feelings,
stretching ambitions,
beginning of something,
beginning of everything...

18th November
Watching me

There is someone watching me,
typing my thoughts
and exposing my feelings,
hanging on my back,
whispering in my ear,
stroking my hair…

there is someone watching me,
drinking coffee to fuel
the words spilling from my brain,
grabbing my leg,
pulling on my arm,
cramping my stomach…

there is someone watching me,
creating worlds from nothing
and then destroying them like nothing,
poking my eyes,
kicking my shins,
shining my glasses…

there is someone watching me,
taking steps too far
into realms of unforgiven,
fanning my desires,
building up my passions,
wanting my fucking.

19th November
Hell Awaits

Boiling blood bubbles and spits,
screeching death carries you on,
hell awaits with eager pain
ready to consume your soul.

Covered in piss and shit (again),
scarred by disappointment in others,
hell awaits with gleeful joy
ready to strip your soul.

Your sins choke you out,
ripping away any respect,
hell awaits with trembling fingers
ready to gorge your soul.

Torn apart by your peers,
savaging faces take their piece,
hell awaits with hungry stomachs
ready to eat your soul.

When all that is left is puss,
oozing brains squashed,
hell awaits with bloated satisfaction
ready to digest your soul.

Then a sudden horror a washes over you,
your eyes open to all around you,
hell doesn't need to await
already here to stay.

20th November
Hot

Thick,
hot,
black,
sweet,
steamy,
tingly,
salty,
bitter,
hard...

it caresses my lips
making them moist,
it warms up my insides
filling me up,
it feels strong in my hands
dangerous and spicy...

I feel alive and awake after my daily fix,
I feel fulfilled and ready for anything,
I feel special and inspired; almost loved...

damn...that coffee is fucking good!!!

(what were you thinking of?!?!?!?!?!)

21st November
Cry

Enough to make you…

memories of future,
hurt and lost,
the reflection of time
pierces; torn,
rain lashes across my face,
streaks of mud drip drop
drip drop drip drop,
fists claw the stones,
scrape up the piss and shit (more),
my skull bangs against; the wall…

fractured…

just another brick,
just another barcode,
just another pay check,
just another nobody,
just another lie,
just another fake,
just another other…

slice away, slice today, slice tomorrow…

cut,
bleed,
rinse,
repeat,
cut,
bleed,
rinse,
repeat…

22nd November
cold

Finger tips tingle and numb,
feelings deep inside far away,
a hard set head decided,
terrorised and disturbed,
the cold air of humanity.

Actions on the 9-5 mean nothing,
a mere process of earning,
issues of amnesia,
or actualities of rinse and repeat,
the cold reality of living.

Manipulation from supposed,
excuses force fed from bullshit,
a disappointment in those,
battered by their lies,
the cold smell of selfish.

Pink skin eager and willing,
heat ready to be drained,
no escape from this,
cornered and raped,
the cold feel of steel.

23rd November Words that pop into my head

Bogies,
aliens,
light,
sore dick,
beep beep (tumble dryer just beeped...back in a few minutes),
coffee,
trampoline...3 hours 39 minutes to go,
combat drop,
bit of sun,
picking my lip,
sounds like the wrath of...
distant clouds,
prog rock underneath my desk,
laptop on top of my desk,
mouse,
phone,
printer,
this is where the magic happens,

lonely...
unhappy...
embarrassed,
hateful,
should be put down...

turtles (heroes in half shell),
too much music (never have too much),
not enough time (never enough time),
regrets forever (can't take them back)
a motor head (a motor heart)
cold, lost, alone, death,
death
death
death
death
death
death.

24th November
Bells

Oceans tumble down from above,
the ever watching eye of the sun blinks,
blinded briefly by the breaking waves
on a crusty white beach singing on an island.

The swaying dance of the trees groove,
shimmering reflections hide their secrets
of serpent dreams and spells,
only one holding on to the inner child can see...

bells.

Calling from a distant patch of green,
surrounded by the voice of the animals,
their soft words beckoning you closer,
an invisible moon watch smiling you on.

Like a man in the rain swimming,
the ding dong has you mesmerized
as beauty draws in all around you,
wrapping its gaze into your soul and whispering...

bells.

The steady beat.
The feeling of one.
The sudden awareness,
far above the clouds...

heart.

25th November
The mighty…

Indeed…he is here,
a double whammy of genius…
coffee at the ready,
time for space time!

Blast off,
silly humans,
destroy the Earth,
flying in solar winds…
wonderful!

What is that farty noise?
No…oh god NO!!!!
Part of me, part of me,
ha ha ha – the ultimate guitar hero,
the ultimate double cross…
nerd!

Look out for the ray of death (wink, wink),
time is not a straight line,
gone, gone away,
watch out for the greys,
watch out for the wandering eye…
raw!

How can you look at me looking at you?
How can you judge my actions through your actions?
How can you look above my head without looking above your own?
You are a puppet.
I am a puppet.
We are all puppets.
Puppets.

26th November
Blankness

It's in their eyes,
the blank stares,
the mute screams,
the laughing waves.

Their ignorance bleeds defeat,
the way they open up closed wounds,
the manner in which words are twisted,
a reunion of past mistakes brought forward.

Doesn't matter if you try your best,
doesn't matter if you give a shit,
doesn't matter that you remain loyal,
doesn't matter that you work hard.

Look into that mirror,
see the piss and shit reflected,
watch the world go on regardless,
smell the two time grime.

Sometimes I just want to drift away,
find a hole and go to sleep,
be done with everyone and all,
be free of everyone and all,
be gone of everyone and all...

amputate the blankness.

27th November
Do you know?

Do you know how I feel?
Do you know, do you know, do you know?

Do you just how I fell?
Do you know what it's like?
Do you know how hard it is to survive?
Do you know, do you know, do you know?

All dead, all dead; mother.
Do you know how I wish it was me instead?
Do you know how I wish we could swap places?
Do you know it was my fault?
Do you know, do you know, do you know?

You don't know, you can't know,
because you weren't there,
you aren't me…you're you,
do you know, do you know, do you know?

Expose me to my core,
there is nothing left,
no fight,
no care,
no shit.

Expose me to my core,
I gave up a long time ago,
merely going through the motions,
merely sticking to the rails,
merely being the puppet
aware of his strings.

28th November
WOW

It may be a black Friday...

...but it's also a force awakening!!!

That is all!!

29th November
Sickness

Sloppy nose
Infected head
Cold fever
Kicking aches
Nails scraping
Entertaining disease
Sore voice
Sorry for me.

30th November
The book

If you could write a book of your life before you
lived it...how would you write it?

Would you write it full of good things and happy things and
butterflies?
Would you be the most popular person?
Would you be the most beautiful person?
Would you be the most successful person?
Would you only have good things happen to you?
Would you give yourself an easy life?
Would you give yourself a disease free life?
Would you give yourself a blessed life?
What would you do?

If you could write a book of your life before you lived it...how
would you REALLY write it?

To have a life full of all the above things would mean you writing
a book of everybody's lives.
The life you have is directly influenced by those who are a part of
your life.
It is not directly influenced by your actions and decisions.
It is based on actions and decisions completely out of your
control.

Besides, your life would be very boring if you wrote it.
It's the unpredictability that gives life its meaning...

good and bad.

1st December
The Last of Us

"So here I am finally ready,
to take on the world and win,
bring light into my every present darkness,
no longer wandering in blind aimlessness."

The stillness hovers over layers of green and brown,
the landscape ripples as far as the eye can see
framed by a sky made up of shades of grey;
eerie yet split within divisions of light.

A silent track shines the odd burst of life,
scattering birds and rabbits in all directions,
skeleton trees sway naked and sharp,
their skin ripped by the oncoming winter.

And I sit alone hacking away at lettered keys,
laughing at my own optimistic bullshit;
"take on the world and win"...never,
infected by a defeat already lost.

My "wandering in blind aimlessness" remains,
the only constant for the last of us
and a reminder that there is no home,
the path long wiped from my memory.

And yet one final hurrah will be set,
a staggering surge of imagination
written by a broken soul; the truth,
an end to the outpouring reality...

this heat, it's hell closing in on me.

2nd December
Living carcass

The bright lights never change
bouncing off the grey sludge,
dragging my feet over a well-trodden path
leads me to the same place...
in the same space...
at the same time...
for the same result...
on the same day.

Clock watching,
repeating dialogue,
a fixed state,
over and over and over,
round and round and round,
repeat, repeat, repeat...
and repeat.

I may as well rip my soul into pieces.

As the days go on,
so my shadow fails,
the madness of doing
the same thing over burns,
a little piece of integrity
falls from my living carcass,
nothing left but a defeated shell
cracked and lifeless; robotic.

time
to
die.

3rd December
All with my...

lack of sleep.
disturbed dreams.
cold fingers.
dark journey.

peppermint and nettle tea.
desk full of shit.
nose full of snot.
depressed feeling.

set up to fall.
attitude of loss.
why the fuck.
screw this.

fuck this..

4th December
cold

fuck me...it's cold!!!

5th December
I still creak…

I still creak…
and I ache.
I tire…
and I weaken.
I frown…
and I crease.
I swallow…
and I drown.
I freeze…
and I stiffen.
I sleep…
and I disturb.
I cough…
and I wheeze.
I see…
and I cry.
I work…
and I despair.
I hurt…
and I ignore.
I touch…
and I soften.
I create…
and I destroy.
I sweet…
and I sour.
I welcome…
and I collapse.
I hope…
and I darken.
I remember…
and I regret.
I live…
and I die…
forever.

6th December
Nightmares

Coughing,
tossing and turning,
the moons light...
dancing shadows and fears.

Waking nightmares
cast their eyes,
digging their fingers
into a tormented mind,
rocking me awake
keeping me from sleep,
smiling disease
infecting twitching body...
take a breath; a deep breath now.

On this island of cold air I sit,
clock watching...tick fucking tock,
channel hopping...flick fucking flick,
on this island of cold air I sit.

Cookies.
Hot drink.
Time.
Bed.
Drift.
Finally...

...up.
Early.
Tired.
Loss.
Bollocks.

7th December
Head's down...

Head's still down...can't keep going.
Head's down...no focus on the job.
Head's down...why plan ahead?
Head's down...what plan?
Head's down...can't understand the task.
Head's down...there is no pay.
Head's down...balls on the chin.
Head's down...I am a mistake.
Head's down...calm?
Head's down...not organised.
Head's down...drink lots of coffee.
Head's down...time is not your friend.
Head's down...remember to hold your breath.
Head's down...guitar?

8th December
The scars

The scars on my arms have faded,
their rivers of blood all dried up,
only a hint of pain remains,
only a hint of mark is left.

The scars on my arms have faded,
not that it means I am healed,
forever a haunting action lingers,
forever a haunting pride is gone.

The scars on my arms have faded,
deep down they burn brightly,
never a quench of thirst free,
never a quench dry is wet.

The scars on my arms have faded,
but on my soul new ones appear,
always a reaction to my pathetic,
always a reaction me is me.

The scars on my arms *may* have faded,
but I can see them as clear as day,
fingering a tale of eternal conflict,
fingering a tale torment is now.

9th [redacted]

Limp…

[redacted]
drained, [redacted]
bring me [redacted]
[redacted]
a desire,
bitter and [redacted]
[redacted] sweat,
fuck me hard,
[redacted] in utter…
…astonishment
and crazed [redacted]
[redacted] darkness
[redacted] amongst
stars in ink,
[redacted] deep,
[redacted] thick,
mirrored sex
our mouths [redacted]
[redacted] melt,
stretched out and fucked…

…a passion, it lingers and sings,
[redacted]
taking with it all rational thought
[redacted]
for that perfect moment that hangs…

…and [redacted]

10th December
Untitled

A frail frame casts a thin shadow,
bent and weak it shuffles on
towards a dark demented crucifixion,
the path covered in broken glass.

A caged and contorted mind
screaming for freedom and redemption,
cathedral of suffering peaked through cut
after cut after cut; deaths desire.

An untitled man
in an untitled life
with an untitled future
tormented by an untitled past.

Unified in pain.
Never rid of it.
Tragic corruption.
It will never stop.
To the end of days.
Lo and behold.
Even into hell.
Deserved of me this is...

Well, it is!

11th December
Is this the real life…or is this just fantasy? →

I wake up full of beans,
having slept a good solid 8 hours
I am ready for the day ahead.

I open the curtains to see a beautiful day,
sit and have a coffee with some toast and cereal,
get showered and dressed for work,
say hello to the neighbours and get in my car.

The drive to work is quiet and easy,
parking into the spot saved for me
I say hello to my fellow colleagues
as I walk to my desk…time for another coffee.

My job is rewarding and meaningful,
I do everything I have planned,
I do it to my best ability,
I make a difference…and so does
everyone else I work with.

The drive home is quiet and easy,
parking into the spot that is mine
I say hello to my neighbours once again
as I walk into my house…time for a healthy dinner.

Spending the rest of the day writing,
spending the rest of the day full of energy,
spending the rest of the day happy,
spending the rest of the day looking
forward to tomorrow.

I go to bed ready for nice dreams,
prepared for another sleepless night,
goodnight everyone and god
bless us all……………………

neither!!

12th December Destruction inbound

It will rise through me,
destruction inbound,
burning strains of goodness
eating that which remains…

the whole ground cracks.

Nothing more than a plaything,
an old broken toy kicked about,
a death star full of fire and hate…

crushed by the weight.

My fallen soul crawls through asphalt rain,
bleeding wrists hissing with painful remorse…

lost to the temptation of despair.

Freedom comes with the ultimate price of endless suffering…

forever tormented by a "what could have been".

What.
Could.
Have.
Been?

13th December
Sorrow

There are times when I wander through a place not of this place but a dark place. Its landscape covered with thick sludge with an aroma of treacle in the cold air. Clouds of black crows dripping with oil circle above whilst mountains impose and claw their way across the horizon. Red eyes watch and blink from every space and crack; burning with desire and hatred, their gaze brings drowsiness and fear.

I am forever urging my body to go forward in the sticky dead ground but am continuously forced backwards towards a truth I do not wish to uncover. I think I see figures in the blinding wind; shadows of enormous colossi stalking this sorrowful land and I begin to question my own sanity. Is this hell? Or is this reality? Have I been forsaken to my own inferno? Or is this merely a dream of sorts?

And as before, I cannot say for sure what existence this is. I stand still on a path, assigned, it seems, to me and me alone. A flickering dying light in a swarming breathless blackness; awash with shit and piss, I am fading...fading...fading. And as my eyes falter, this dark place becomes me. It pumps through my veins and fills my lungs. It deafens my ears and cages my heart. It seeps into my bones and rips apart my mind. And finally, with a thunderous mighty noise, earth splitting and painfully sharp; my soul cracks.

Time stops. Cruel clarity bestows upon my final thought and the truth is revealed................and then lost, leaving behind a sorrow...and a single tear.

14th December
A dic

The need for more,
blind impulse,
give it to me.

No rational thought!
Addictions overcome any,
the desire is to great,
painfully (or pleasure?),
twisting any sanity,
distorting all time,
this jilted poison,
the coming relief,
an orgasm of
a personal fucked up vice.

Then comes the high…five.

To hell with all consequence,
who cares about the hurt (or getting caught),
addicted to the itch,
addicted to the scratch,
addicted to the rinse and repeat…

rinse and repeat
rinse and repeat
rinse and fucking repeat.

15th December
The battle of the five armies

Kicked ass!!!

16th December
a fool...part 2

I can see tomorrow,
I can see my world to come,
I can see tomorrow...

a fool to think I matter,
a fool to think I am important,
a fool to think I make a difference...

step on me, squish me like a bug,
squeeze the life out of me...

forget what I have done,
forget who I am,
forget me,
forget...

my life...I've been waiting
for this moment to come
for I can see tomorrow,
I can see my world to be,
a brave new world you see...

...2015...or maybe 2016.

17th December
Dust

Still there amongst the dead skin,

cradling in a dark corner,

a mind cracked,

a body smashed,

screaming with anguish,

out of reach...forever..................................?

18th December
the prawn curry and the toffee sticky pudding

Indeed...yes...yum yum!

19th December
there is a loss

Up on time,
desire drifting away,
same trip, same scenery,
same same; loss.

Never boring,
not the point,
constant struggle,
outer strength; loss.

That connection,
unspoken wanton,
passion exposed,
not to be; loss.

Mere words,
no meaning,
what happened,
lack of inspiration; loss.

What's out there,
different from in here,
endless possibilities,
there is a; loss.

20th December
all you need is six lines part 32

the settling glass
a shattered corpse
revealing reflective memories
two zero one four
is there to be many more?
breathless is my internal war.

21st December
p pii CK

I wwwannnnaaaa......

cleave ((((ccllllllEEEE aave) YOuR

FUCKING FUCKING FUCKING...

...face in....wait, no I don't!!

Not anymore because I don't live next door to you, you fucking slag!!

Noooo longer p pii CK

AT YOuR brAiNssssssssssss –

OR

www aLL oww

IINNNNN

YOuR

bbbbbblllllllooooooddddddddd............

although, it would be cool to do the tango
with your butchered corpse!!!!!!

22nd December
a blank space

Sometimes I just stare...

well, in fact, I do a lot of staring...

you know – into space...

with a blank look on my face...

lost, tormented, dead.

23rd December
Dunno?!

So, in work today. Asked if we could go early tomorrow seen as it being Christmas Eve and all...was told no. Ok, I said, what about if we come in early and finish early thus still doing the same amount of hours...was told no. Everyone else finishes at 3pm. People working day shift have to stay till 5pm...on Christmas FUCKING Eve. So, all I did today was:

Handling various objects
and stroking my stubble.
Scratching my back
and tapping my feet.
Fingering the mouse
and stroking the keyboard.

24th December
Christmas Eve

Christmas Eve two zero one four,
stuck in work once more,
can't wait to get out that door,
Christmas Eve two zero one four.

Christmas Eve a windy cold day,
a bright one indeed they say,
now let us all pray,
Christmas Eve a windy cold day.

Christmas Eve typing fresh words,
dark now no more birds,
my writing full or turds,
Christmas Eve typing fresh words.

Christmas Eve Ulysses 31 here we come,
series not far from being done,
god I love it so much fun,
Christmas Eve Ulysses 31 here we come.

Christmas Eve two zero one four,
wonder how it differs from before,
Santa dropping off a PS4,
Christmas Eve two zero one four.

25th December
Christmas Day

Floating down the endless river
the sky full of bloodstone and diamonds,
heading towards a skeletal domain,
this unexpected journey's end.

Far away isolated and alien
the evil within shines,
I am my own Frankenstein's monster,
hear my cry quake forever.

And so I transform into nothing,
my two towers of strength weep,
lost soul now part of the walking dead,
and now I sail into the black.

26th December
I wanna ride

I just wanna ride,
deep and fulfilled,
I just wanna ride,
send me to heaven,
I just wanna ride,
make me come,
I just wanna ride,
is it so wrong?

27th December
a dull pain

there it is, in my chest,
but not just in my chest...my mind,
it swims through my body,
infects my blood; a disease.

clenching numb fingers,
toes feel cold and dead,
muscles weak and lost
where is my strength?

my bones hurt,
black and brittle,
they creak and split,
marrow dried up and dust.

I can't think straight,
I can't see straight,
I can't breathe straight,
I can't remember straight.

a dull pain,
keeps the strings tight,
silences the voice,
locks the chains...
release me!

28th December in a home

There is a building made of bricks and stone,
full of past lives both lost and won,
a building made of wood and nails,
full of the most wonderful tales.

Adventures spread across the globe,
battles fought and secrets sold,
daring deeds of love and desire,
burning the midnight sun on a funeral pyre.

Living life like there was no tomorrow,
no time for pain, no time for sorrow,
not a single soul could hold you back,
ebb and flow you knew the crack.

But then you came to this building made of bricks and stone,
this is where you eventually end up in a home,
this sad looking building made of wood and nails,
how did it come to this, how did you fail?

29th December
end of the line – part 1

The drone of filling a space
With a handful of bodies and machines
Cold air houses cold steel
Brings cold plastic

"Let's break up the fun
For the sake of a few days off"
Said the bastards of contradiction
Head up their own fuckholes

They rant and they rave
Bring the house down every day
Rules and paperwork
A religion to them and theirs

Nodding in the blindness
Pissing from swirly eyes
The biggest puppets of them all
Floppy do floppy do wop

Behold the power of figures
"The workers aren't doing enough"
The numbers dictate our sex
"The bosses aren't getting enough"

And we shuffle and we sick
Follow without question
Although question we dare
Our barcodes ripped from us

End of the line for me
Too many soul pieces lost
It's what I see from inside
The drone of filling a space

30th December
end of the line – part 2

About writing, that wonderful thing,
it turns and twists and soars,
fuelled by the life in-between,
(coffee is the ink that fills our minds and colours our words)
It can cast you as the star, the hero,
or the tortured villain, the antihero,
the sex god or the one on the receiving end,
(our bodies are ours to give to anyone at any time)

Nothing can limit the extent of imagination, away,
an ecliptic perpendicular roar of wonder,
impossibility isn't even a word,
(cages built are purely by design of fear only)

And the many sounds that inspire, that soundtrack,
forces air into the lungs of letters,
sending them to another level of meaning,
(moods and feelings dancing over a blank page)

So this experiment draws close, end of the line,
a spiced up juicy diary of sorts,
turning the norm into the abnorm,
(a final flourish into the abyss my dear friends)

31st December
end of the line – part 3

Two zero one four…end of the line,
another year is over, waste of time?

I said goodbye to a dear friend,
it had to come though, it had to end.

I eventually embraced a new home,
still at times I feel utterly alone.

I got lost on a space trip of awe,
Interstellar exposed my mind raw.

I became less of a man to Sanko,
more a number at their disposal.

I expanded my writing topics tenfold,
some are daring extremely bold.

I continue to realise she is too good,
Michelle will soon see that I'm a dud.

I sense my fantasies getting stronger,
the feelings lasting a lot longer.

I awed at the return of Ziltoid,
his music could move a droid.

I played outside with Nikki's kids,
a little bit of innocence returned it did.

I explored all the poetry signs,
all you need sometimes is six lines.

I added a few new fresh cuts,
the need diminishing with luck.

And so I ask once more,
two zero one four...end of the line,
another year over no longer mine,
was it all just a big waste of time?!

Two zero one five...let's see...
this heat, it's hell closing in on me.

FINISHED

epilogue – end of the line (part 4)

The strain was immense. "Remember to breathe my son", a voice softly says into his ear as the ship shakes from side to side with a violent vendetta. "This is it, we are nearly there" whispers the same voice, "end of the line". The ship begins to barrel role as it breaks through the Earth's atmosphere and the heat is now at dangerous levels when suddenly a warning light flashes on and sparks erupts from the console. Gritting his teeth under his breath he mumbles "Come on K.A.R.A. just get me to the surface...please", to which the ship replies, "Malfunction, malfunction...deploying air brakes...........now". An ear piercing squeal and the sound of metal bending levels out the ship and slows it down just before it hits the ground and buries its nose into the wasteland of the Earth. There is a popping noise as the hatch opens up and sunlight streams in setting fire to the interior instantaneously, "Good.... luck.......my...............don't forget.........the amaze............ ing....................frog" and with a final spark, the console dies. Fighting through the flames, he jumps out of the ship and knocks the wind completely out of him. Breathe, breathe in the air... (To be continued).

James S M Parker 14/02/16

thanks

Once again, my true love and thanks go to my Michelle – still here, still with me, still loving me, still supporting me. xxx

And to my cat Leia, who constantly wakes me in the middle of the night and leaves little pooh presents around the house. xxx

My family, close friends and social network fanatics remain the same...massive thank you to them just for being who you are. A special mention must go to my former employee, Sanko Gosei, who made me redundant after 16 years of service with no warning, no real reason and no remorse...thank you for freeing me and paying me out a decent amount of money therefore allowing me to self-publish this, my second book.

My new neighbours out here in Halsall – Nikki and Emma especially. xxx But more so to their children, Mac, Kennedy, Kara and Logan...playing with them, talking to them and being a part of their lives has made me feel younger and more alive than I ever have and almost makes me want to have my own children. Thanks to Harrison and Taylor as well.

An extra special thank you goes to Kara who planted the seed for my next project. Listening to you talk, sharing our writings and experiencing your talent as an author has lifted my spirits and inspired my own work.

Thanks again to Grosvenor for their help, support and professionalism, working with you again has been a pleasure.

I am hoping that this book (coupled with my first) will be a testament and release for all the bad things that have happened over the last 20 years. I am who I am and can't change how the past has affected my present and how it will continue to affect my future... however, this is now the time to create new worlds outside of my own and actually live a little.

Next – time to delve into the world of children books...wish me luck!!!

And yes, a final thank you to you, the reader – 14/02/16.

tweet – @absinthe666

inbrokenthoughts.blogspot.co.uk

Lightning Source UK Ltd.
Milton Keynes UK
UKOW02f1129080516

273789UK00001B/11/P

9 781786 23724